Anger Management for the Twenty-First Century

Eight Anger Control Tools to Learn Before It's Too Late!

By Anthony Fiore, Ph.D. and Ari Novick, Ph.D.

Anger Management for the Twenty-First Century

Copyright © 2005 by Century Anger Management

All rights reserved. No part of this book may be used or reproduced in any manner whatsoever without written permission from the publisher.

Book and Cover Design by Julia Martin at Gradient Groove Design (www.gradientgroove.com)
Photographs and Illustrations provided by www.clipart.com

ISBN 0-9768940-0-9

ACKNOWLEDGEMENTS

This book is dedicated to the hundreds of men, women, and teens who have participated in our anger management classes in Southern California and openly shared their struggles in gaining control over their angry feelings with their partners, their families, in the workplace, and on the freeways. Their many contributions and suggestions were incorporated into this material and their success stories motivated us to continue our work.

Many thanks to Roger C. Parker, personal and business coach, author and friend, who from across the country in New Hampshire provided guidance, wisdom, and inspiration to this project and constantly reminded us of the value of our work to all the angry people in the world – and their victims.

We wish to thank and express appreciation for the obvious talents of Julia Martin of Gradient Groove Design and Illustration for designing and editing this book.

Tony would like to say: Many thanks to my significant other Pamela Scavella who supported this project tirelessly and week after week provided administrative support and assistance for our anger management clients. She lovingly assumed much of our daily "life-load" for a long time, freeing my time to devote to this project.

Ari would like to say: Thank you to my wife, Kim Novick, for her unending support, love and encouragement. The countless nights she spent listening to me and giving me the support I needed have been priceless. I would also like to thank Robert Hohenstein, Ph.D., my mentor and friend, for encouraging me and supporting me over the last several years. Your support and belief in my goals has helped me tremendously. I would also like to thank my partner Tony Fiore, Ph.D. for working so hard and collaboratively to create this workbook together. Finally, I would like to thank my parents Gerald Novick, DDS and Eleanor Novick, Ph.D. for their love, support, and belief in my abilities.

Table of Contents

Click black button to proceed to requested page.

"Anyone can be angry, that is easy.
But to be angry with the right person, to the right degree,
at the right time, for the right reason,
and in the right way, this is not easy."

– Aristotle (384-322 B.C.)

Anger Management for the 21st Century
Introduction

> *One just has to read the daily newspaper or watch the evening news to conclude that controlling one's angry feelings is a major challenge for many adults, teens, and children.*

Who Can Benefit from this Book?

It seems that anger is everywhere in our society. One just has to read the daily newspaper or watch the evening news to conclude that controlling one's angry feelings is a major challenge for many adults, teens, and children.

Uncontrolled anger is a major factor in domestic violence and spousal abuse, in aggressive driving violations, in workplace rudeness and disruption, in marital conflicts, and in family fights.

Recent research also shows that anger is very bad for health and general well-being. Angry people apparently have shorter life spans and are ill more often than other people.

This book is intended to be a self-help manual for adults who need specific tools to help control or manage their anger. These skills can successfully be applied in the workplace, in relationships, while driving, with one's family, or in any other situation in which anger control is an issue.

This manual is also intended to be used as a workbook by anger management facilitators in various settings or by individual therapists who use a structured approach to therapy and need a week by week guide with homework assignments for their clients.

How do you feel when you are angry?

Check all that apply to you:

- ❏ Anxious
- ❏ Worthless
- ❏ Hostile
- ❏ Depressed
- ❏ Mean/evil
- ❏ Bitter
- ❏ Bitchy
- ❏ Numb
- ❏ Furious
- ❏ Revengeful
- ❏ Rebellious
- ❏ Paranoid
- ❏ Victimized
- ❏ Sarcastic
- ❏ Resentful
- ❏ Frustrated
- ❏ Irritated
- ❏ Enraged
- ❏ Loathing
- ❏ Destructive
- ❏ Disgusted
- ❏ Contemptuous
- ❏ Spiteful
- ❏ Grumpy
- ❏ Outraged
- ❏ Jealous
- ❏ Aggravated

Our View of Anger: Anger Is Normal

We view angry feelings as a normal emotional reaction to frustration in our every day world. It is natural to become angry when we have a goal and this goal is blocked in some way. Most of the time we do not choose to be angry, but somehow we are suddenly in the feeling. Often, we don't even know we are angry until we feel it.

Anger, which comes from a part of our brain that is very old can be brief, lasting only a second or two. You can be happy one moment and angry the next.

Angry feelings may also continue over a long period of time. If you are angry a lot, but your feelings are not connected to life circumstances, we call it a "mood." Angry moods lead to angry feelings coming on stronger and faster.

Once anger begins, it generates changes in our expressions, our faces, our voices, and in the way we think. It also creates impulses to action. Sometimes we have thoughts that generate anger. Other times we have thoughts that occur at the same time as anger. It is also possible for your anger to generate thoughts about what you are angry toward.

Anger isn't just one emotion, but a family of emotions that are related to each other both in our brains and in our behavior. People often give a variety of names to their angry feelings, which range from mild irritation to rage.

Scientists tell us that the purpose of emotions such as anger is to organize and mobilize all of our bodily systems to respond to our environment in some way.

This happens even when we are not aware of it. When we are aware of the emotion, it becomes a "feeling" that is felt somewhere in our body. In fact, emotions in the anger family are probably a "hard-wired" survival mechanism in our brain that has been part of the human race for millions of years to protect us from enemies and to ensure that we continue to exist.

To help understand this in more detail, we need to look at how our brain works. To view it simply, among many other parts, we have an "emotional" part of our brain and a "thinking" part of our brain.

Anger, like most emotions, is regulated by that section of the brain called the "limbic system." Emotional memories are stored in a structure called the "amygdala" and other structures located in the limbic system.

www.centuryangermanagement.com / Copyright 2005

Because of the amygdala and other structures in your brain, you may experience anger now in your life that may actually be caused by a mixture of what is triggering it now and experiences you have had in the past. This "old anger" is activated by your brain in its attempt to protect you. Neuroscientists call this "implicit memory"—meaning that we can experience the effects of a memory without even realizing that it is a memory that we are having.

It is up to the thinking part of the brain, our frontal lobes, to find a way to deal with the angry feelings that the amygdala and other brain structures have set in motion. As thinking human beings we have the unique ability among species to have choices regarding how we will deal with our feelings.

> *Anger isn't just one emotion, but a family of emotions that are related to each other both in our brains and in our behavior.*

Anger Can Be Positive

Anger is an emotion that is normal to all of us. Usually, anger is a recognition that we have been hurt or feel threatened. It is a warning signal and a clear indication that something is wrong. This may be a signal to make a clear decision to protect yourself.

Anger is a healthy release. It takes an enormous amount of energy to hold anger inside, which may cause fatigue, boredom, and physical illness. If you release your anger appropriately, you may find that you develop healthier relationships.

Example: *You have a friend that is constantly late. This is very upsetting to you, but you do saying anything? No, you just begin to make excuses not to see your friend. You may lose a valuable friendship. If you are able to tell your friend that being late is difficult for you and makes you feel unimportant, she may decide that she values your honesty, apologizes, and begins to arrive on time. This interaction may facilitate a closer relationship with your friend.*

Positive use of anger can also build self-esteem. If you are able to tell someone your feelings instead of keeping them inside, you are saying to the world, "I am a valuable person and I expect to be treated as such."

When Does Anger Become A Problem?

Anger expression can be viewed as a behavior, and like all behavior, it has a purpose. Another way to say this is when we get angry we are usually tying to accomplish some goal—like getting somebody to do something, or to be heard, or to solve a problem, or to get one or more of our needs met.

The only problem is that anger rarely is effective in getting us what we want—perhaps 95% of the time it actually makes things worse.

Anger management IS NOT about never getting angry, which would be an unrealistic (and probably undesirable) goal given how our brains are "wired." Rather, anger management is about finding other more positive ways to communicate or behave so that you become a more effective and satisfied person who has better relationships with other people.

If anger is sometimes positive but most of the time is not so positive, how can you tell if it is a problem for you?

The short answer is that anger is a problem for you if the "cost" of it is greater than the benefit you get from it!

> **"Often, people try to repair the damage they created with angry outbursts or irrational anger, but this takes a great deal of time, if it works at all."**

What are Some of the Costs of Your Anger?

Cost #1 – Your Health

In one study reported by *The Harvard Mental Health Newsletter,* people with normal blood pressure who scored high on a rating scale for anger were nearly three times more likely to have a heart attack or require bypass surgery within five years.

Another study, published in the *American Heart Association Journal Circulation* showed that hotheaded men who explode with anger seem to be at greater risk of having a stroke or dying.

Cost #2 – Your Self-Esteem

While some people feel justified in getting angry, most people simply don't like themselves very much if their anger is too intense, if it is too frequent, or if it lasts too long. During an outburst, you may actually feel good, but afterwards when you return to normal you may begin to feel guilty or have remorse for the outburst, especially if you can see the negative effect it has had on people in your life.

Cost #3 – Your Relationships

This is usually one of the heaviest costs of anger—disruption or loss of relationships or loss of respect with people in your life that are important to you. This is especially true if your anger reaches the point of turning to physical aggression. In fact, the most frequent reason for people to attend anger management classes is to salvage a relationship, usually with a spouse or partner, but also with a parent or a child before it is too late.

> *To empathize is to see with the eyes of another, to hear with the ears of another, and to feel with the heart of another.*

It is difficult for a relationship of any kind to survive very long in an atmosphere of anger or similar emotions. Explosive anger creates fear and emotional distance in others. Simmering anger creates an extremely tense atmosphere devoid of trust and openness.

Often, people try to repair the damage they created with angry outbursts or irrational anger, but this takes a great deal of time, if it works at all. It is usually not easy for your partner or family member to recover from a major assault from you – even if it is only on a verbal level. You may feel better after the explosion, but the other person is then left with all that negative feeling. Remember, you can't "unring" a bell. Once you explode, that image stays with other people for a long time.

If anger turns to aggression or violence, the consequences are even more severe. Several influential studies have shown that one-third of couples experienced at least one incident of domestic violence during the course of their marriage. The same study found that about 1,500,000 children per year are severely assaulted (kicked, punched, beaten up, or burned) in their homes.

Cost #4 – Your Children

The effect of children witnessing extreme conflict in the home can be devastating – more harmful most of the time than a parental divorce.

- *It is estimated that between 2.3 million and 10 million children are exposed to intimate partner violence each year in the United States.*

- *Although many adults believe they have protected their children from exposure to domestic violence, 80-90% of children in those homes can give detailed descriptions of the violence experienced in their families.*

- *The detrimental effects of intimate partner violence on children have been clearly established through research studies and observations of adult survivors in domestic violence programs.*

Cost #5 – The Workplace

There is no question that poorly handled anger, frustration and resentment sabotage workplace productivity. Studies show that up to 42% of employee time is spent engaging in or trying to resolve conflict. This results in wasted employee time, mistakes, stress, lower morale, hampered performance, and reduced profits and/or service.

> *Anger expressed toward others is often a misguided way of communicating a feeling we have or a need that is not being satisfied by other people or situations.*

Other studies show even more disturbing results of anger in the workplace: for instance, it is estimated that workplace violence costs $4.2 billion each year in the United States alone. According to the Bureau of Justice Statistics, about 500,000 victims of violent crime in the workplace lose an estimated 1.8 million workdays each year.

The Core Eight Anger Management Skills

This workbook is organized around eight core skills of anger management that the authors have found to be extremely effective for both voluntary and court-ordered participants of anger management classes in Southern California.

Tool #1– Recognize Stress

Stress is often the *trigger* that takes us from feeling peaceful to experiencing uncomfortable angry feelings in many common life situations. Whether the stressor is external or internal, scientists have discovered that the major systems of the body work together to provide one of the human organism's most powerful and sophisticated defenses: the stress response that you may know as "fight, flight, or freeze." Before your stress response turns into anger or aggression, use stress management strategies to get it under control.

Tool #2 – Develop Empathy

To empathize is to see with the eyes of another, to hear with the ears of another, and to feel with the heart of another. Lack of empathy leads to poor communication and a failure to understand others. To manage anger, it often helps to see our anger as a combination of other people's behavior and our lack of empathy.

Tool #3 – Respond Instead of React

Many times we become angry because we find people and situations that literally "push our buttons," and we react just like a jukebox that automatically pulls down a record and starts playing when you make a selection. Rather than reacting to anger triggers in this fashion, you can learn to *choose* how to deal with frustrating situations—to *respond* rather than automatically react like that jukebox.

> *Anger is often triggered by a discrepancy between what we expect and what we get.*

Tool #4 – Change that Conversation with Yourself

What you tell yourself is what you get. We are constantly having inner conversations—also called "self-talk"—that create, decrease, or intensify our feelings and emotional states, including anger. Learning to recognize and modify that conversation is an important tool in anger control.

Tool #5 – Communicate Assertively

Anger expressed toward others is often a misguided way of communicating a feeling we have or a need that is not being satisfied by other people or situations. Assertive communication is a set of skills to teach you how to honestly and effectively communicate how you feel and how you are responding to things without getting angry or hostile about it.

Tool #6 – Adjust Expectations

Anger is often triggered by a discrepancy between what we expect and what we get. Learning to adjust those expectations—sometimes upward and other times downward—can help us cope with difficult situations or people, or even cope with ourselves. There are four ways to adjust those expectations that are simple thought-skills to acquire.

Tool #7 – Forgive, but Don't Forget!

Anger is often the result of grievances we hold toward other people or situations, usually because of our perception and feeling of having been wronged by them in some way. Resentment is a form of anger that does more damage to the holder than the offender. Making the decision to "let go" (while still protecting ourselves) is often a process of forgiveness—or at least acceptance—and a major step toward anger control.

Tool #8 – Retreat and Think Things Over!

Research shows that we are pretty much incapable of resolving conflicts or thinking rationally in an argument when our stress level reaches a certain point. To avoid losing control either physically or verbally, it is often best to take a temporary "time-out" and leave. This tool of anger management works much better if (a) you commit to return within a reasonable amount of time to work things out, and (b) you work on your "self-talk" while trying to cool down.

Anger History Inventory

This inventory should be completed at the start of your anger management program and then reviewed later so you can see to what extent your thinking, feelings, and behavior have changed as you practice and apply the eight tools of anger control.

1. Please describe the incident or reasons why you decided you needed help with your anger or why you enrolled in an anger management program.

_____

_____

_____

_____

2. As you think back now to what happened, what was it you really wanted to happen in that situation?

_____

_____

_____

_____

3. Anger is a form of communication. Why did you think that communicating in an angry way would get you what you wanted or needed?

_____

_____

_____

_____

4. Often anger is triggered by other emotions such as fear, frustration, or feeling overwhelmed. What feelings were you having?

_____

_____

_____

_____

5. Were you able to take some responsibility for your anger, or did you see it as entirely
   the fault of someone else?

_____

_____

_____

_____

6. What was the "cost" of your anger? This can be expressed in terms of emotional costs,
   financial costs, legal costs, relationship costs, or job costs.

• On you _____

_____

_____

• On your family _____

_____

_____

• On others _____

_____

_____

7. Do you have a past history of angry or aggressive behavior?
   Did you grow up in a violent or angry home?

_____

_____

_____

8. How could you have handled the situation better?

_____

_____

_____

_____

_____

NOTES

_____

_____

_____

_____

_____

_____

_____

_____

_____

_____

_____

_____

_____

_____

_____

_____

_____

_____

_____

_____

_____

_____

Anger Control Tool #1
Dealing with Stress

One of the major challenges of living and thriving in current times is managing our stress levels in a complex world with many demands and expectations.

We often receive phone calls with the other voice on the line saying something like, "Sir, I need some help with my anger, I think my wife is going to leave me if I don't do something about this." The voice continues, "I am a really nice guy, most of the time, but I just 'lost it' the other night and yelled at my wife calling her horrible things." He continues, "I don't know how to deal with all my stress and I am becoming a monster…" Our reply is often calming, as we know that learning stress management techniques, in conjunction with other skills, can greatly reduce one's level of anger, anxiety, and stress.

Stress and anger tend to go hand and hand. The higher one's stress level the easier it is to allow our anger to get out of control. Participants in our classes have often said they don't always know what causes their stress. The creation of stress is a simple equation. Stress is created when we have more demands than resources to meet those demands. For example, if you have to buy gifts for ten people and you only have time to shop for five of them this can create stress. Learning stress management techniques is an effective way to reduce the physical, behavioral, and emotional symptoms caused by stress.

One of the major challenges of living and thriving in current times is managing our stress levels in a complex world with many demands and expectations. Small daily hassles such as getting our children to school on time can add greatly to our level of stress. We can also feel stressed over much larger concerns such as future terrorist attacks on our country or becoming disabled or ill.

Now, let's see how stressors affect your personal physical health

I experience the following:

Have headaches
- ☐ **Never**
- ☐ **Sometimes**
- ☐ **Frequently**

Eat too much
- ☐ **Never**
- ☐ **Sometimes**
- ☐ **Frequently**

Feel tired, fatigued
- ☐ **Never**
- ☐ **Sometimes**
- ☐ **Frequently**

Grinding teeth
- ☐ **Never**
- ☐ **Sometimes**
- ☐ **Frequently**

Chest pains
- ☐ **Never**
- ☐ **Sometimes**
- ☐ **Frequently**

Shortness of breath
- ☐ **Never**
- ☐ **Sometimes**
- ☐ **Frequently**

Heart pounding
- ☐ **Never**
- ☐ **Sometimes**
- ☐ **Frequently**

Sweating
- ☐ **Never**
- ☐ **Sometimes**
- ☐ **Frequently**

Stress and Your Physical Health

The effect of stress on your health can be significant. For instance, a recent study that appeared in the *American Journal of Industrial Medicine* showed that people who lost a job due to retirement age were more than twice as likely to have a stroke as people of the same age who had not lost a job.

People suffering from intense ongoing work or personal stress may develop other cardiovascular problems, such as heart attacks or "hardening of the arteries." Chronic stress can take a toll also on the immune system, making you more susceptible to colds and infections; according to recent research, stress can also ratchet up the immune response to detrimental levels, resulting in allergies, asthma, and autoimmune conditions.

Other stress-related illnesses include diabetes, colitis, chronic fatigue syndrome, fibromyalgia, eczema, and ulcers. Amazingly, new research shows that long-term unrelenting stress on mothers can damage the DNA of their immune-system cells in way that may speed up the aging process.

A famous stress test developed in 1967, called the "Social Re-Adjustment Scale," was designed to predict physical illness based on the number of "Life-Change Units" currently in one's life. For instance, at the top of the list of life events that cause stress is "death of a spouse" (100 units) and "divorce" (60 units). At the bottom of the list are life events such as "vacation" (10 units) and "minor violation of the law" (10 units). The higher your score on this test, the more likely you are to develop a major physical illness in the next two years. You can take this test yourself – it is reproduced for you at the end of this manual in Appendix 1.

Stress and Your Mental Health

Stress also contributes directly or indirectly to many common mental health conditions. Probably the most common are anxiety and depressive disorders and problems. In one study, two-thirds of subjects who experienced a stressful situation had nearly six times the risk of developing depression within a month.

Anxiety disorders are extremely common and are frequently brought on by work and personal stress. Common indications of anxiety disorders include irritability, inability to concentrate or relax, insomnia, and a sense of fear. Many times people also have physical symptoms with their anxiety including nausea, heart

How do stressors affect your mental health?

I experience the following:

Feel irritable
- ☐ **Never**
- ☐ **Sometimes**
- ☐ **Frequently**

Feel unmotivated
- ☐ **Never**
- ☐ **Sometimes**
- ☐ **Frequently**

Feel sad
- ☐ **Never**
- ☐ **Sometimes**
- ☐ **Frequently**

Can't concentrate
- ☐ **Never**
- ☐ **Sometimes**
- ☐ **Frequently**

Feel anger, resentment
- ☐ **Never**
- ☐ **Sometimes**
- ☐ **Frequently**

Feel tense, nervous, anxious, apprehensive
- ☐ **Never**
- ☐ **Sometimes**
- ☐ **Frequently**

Worry a lot
- ☐ **Never**
- ☐ **Sometimes**
- ☐ **Frequently**

Snap at people
- ☐ **Never**
- ☐ **Sometimes**
- ☐ **Frequently**

Overly sensitive
- ☐ **Never**
- ☐ **Sometimes**
- ☐ **Frequently**

Mood swings
- ☐ **Never**
- ☐ **Sometimes**
- ☐ **Frequently**

Procrastinate
- ☐ **Never**
- ☐ **Sometimes**
- ☐ **Frequently**

Quick to argue
- ☐ **Never**
- ☐ **Sometimes**
- ☐ **Frequently**

---

palpitations, muscle tension, sweating, hyperventilation, panic, and bowel disturbances.

Depression is a disorder of mood and emotions that has a strong stress component. Often depressed people do not realize they are depressed because they get used to feeling sad with little joy or capacity to experience life's pleasures. Resentment, anger, and irritability are commonly a part of depression. Depressed people often feel hopeless or helpless, feelings made worse by stressful events in their lives that they have difficulty coping with.

Stress and The Workplace

Stress-related mental health issues are a major concern in the workplace. Studying the trend in the insurance industry in the United States, MetLife published a report in 2003 indicating that psychiatric claims make up 7% of all MetLife's short-term disability claims; the majority of these claims are related to depression (55%) and stress or anxiety (30%). Collectively, the report concludes that these conditions may cost U.S. employers an estimated $344 billion each year due to lost productivity and medical fees, among other reasons.

In addition:
- One fourth of employees view their jobs as the number one stressor in their lives (Northwestern National Life).

- Three fourths believe the worker has more on-the-job stress than a generation ago (Princeton Survey Research Associates).

- Problems at work are more strongly associated with health complaints than any other life stressor – more so than even financial problems or family problems (St. Paul Fire and Marine Insurance Co).

What *IS* Stress?

Stress is a bodily response to life demands, called stressors. This means that your body stresses whenever a demand or requirement is made of you, and you respond to it.

This definition highlights one of the most important things to know about stress and stressors: what may be extremely stressful to you may not affect other people at all because of your different bodily responses to the same "stressor."

You may have better resources to cope with an irritating co-worker;

What Kinds of Workplace Stress Symptoms Do You Experience?

I experience the following:

Poor job performance
- [ ] **Never**
- [ ] **Sometimes**
- [ ] **Frequently**

Poor work focus
- [ ] **Never**
- [ ] **Sometimes**
- [ ] **Frequently**

Unmotivated at job
- [ ] **Never**
- [ ] **Sometimes**
- [ ] **Frequently**

Conflict with supervisors
- [ ] **Never**
- [ ] **Sometimes**
- [ ] **Frequently**

Conflict with co-workers
- [ ] **Never**
- [ ] **Sometimes**
- [ ] **Frequently**

Attendance/tardiness
- [ ] **Never**
- [ ] **Sometimes**
- [ ] **Frequently**

Isolation from peers
- [ ] **Never**
- [ ] **Sometimes**
- [ ] **Frequently**

in this case, the co-worker would be much more of a stressor for you than for other people on your job.

On the other hand, you may have better resources to deal with extreme time pressure to complete a project. In that situation, the boss putting "pressure" on you to complete something would not constitute a stressor for you, but may be very stressful for your co-workers.

For a potential stressor to be a personal stressor we have to first perceive it or experience it as such. This involves both memory and emotion. According to many scientists, for us to perceive an event as stressful we must first remember that it, or something like it, has caused us trouble in the past. These memories are stored in a part of our brain called the "limbic system"; the human brain is particularly good at storing memories with strong emotional content.

Stressors Can Be External or Internal

Sometimes the potential stressor may originate outside of ourselves and other times the potential stressor may be within either our own bodies or minds.

External stressors include job demands, the degree to which you can make your own decisions about your job or tasks, your physical environment (noise, air quality, etc), marital conflict, parenting challenges, daily commutes, financial pressures, and excessive demands on your time.

Internal stressors can be physical (like fatigue or illness) or psychological. Psychological stressors include job dissatisfaction, having negative feelings about your life in general, or holding resentments toward others. Other examples of internal stresses include feeling inadequate or inferior to people around you, or worrying excessively about your life.

Stress May Be Positive

Stress can have many positive effects, such as challenging us to perform at higher levels, motivating us, keeping us at our peak, and focusing our thoughts and behaviors to reach an important goal or objective. This is especially true if our stressors are "acute" – this means that they occur, our bodies respond, we successfully cope, and then we return to normal.

In fact, according to *The American Institute of Stress,* recent studies

What Triggers Most of Your Stress?

Source of Stress:

Family
- ☐ **None**
- ☐ **Some**
- ☐ **Most**

Work / Job
- ☐ **None**
- ☐ **Some**
- ☐ **Most**

Marriage / Relationship
- ☐ **None**
- ☐ **Some**
- ☐ **Most**

Finances
- ☐ **None**
- ☐ **Some**
- ☐ **Most**

Health
- ☐ **None**
- ☐ **Some**
- ☐ **Most**

Life overload
- ☐ **None**
- ☐ **Some**
- ☐ **Most**

Time pressure
- ☐ **None**
- ☐ **Some**
- ☐ **Most**

Not meeting life's goals
- ☐ **None**
- ☐ **Some**
- ☐ **Most**

Disappointment in self
- ☐ **None**
- ☐ **Some**
- ☐ **Most**

Other
- ☐ **None**
- ☐ **Some**
- ☐ **Most**

suggest that short bouts of stress actually increase the immune system's ability to ward off infections and promote wound healing.

However, if acute stressors occur too frequently or are too intense, we may lack the resources to cope. Under these circumstances, we may become overwhelmed and enter a state that some scientists are calling being "stressed-out" as opposed to just being "stressed."

Stressed vs. Stressed-Out

Why do we have undesirable results of stress when stressors in our life become too much for us? The function of the stress response, after all, is NOT to cause illness or problems for us. Rather, most scientists feel that the fight-or-flight response evolved with the objective of ensuring survival and safety.

When things are normal, our powerful stress-response system sharpens our attention and mobilizes our bodies to cope with life events that we perceive as threatening. We cope, our bodies return to normal, and we go on with our lives.

But if stress for us is chronic or overpowering, then our system becomes overwhelmed or derailed; our stress response causes problems for us – either medical, emotional or behavioral problems. In short, we become "stressed-out" or overloaded. When this happens often enough, our smooth running and protective stress system runs amuck contributing to numerous diseases and disorders that affect our bodies, our minds, our emotions, and our behaviors.

The Stress Response

Whether the stressor is external or internal, scientists have discovered that the major systems of the body work together to provide one of it's most powerful and sophisticated defenses: the stress response you may know as the "fight, flight, or freeze" response.

This response helps you to cope with changes or demands in your personal life, in your family, or in the workplace. To do so, it activates and coordinates the brain, glands, hormones, immune system, heart, blood, and lungs. Your natural stress response provides the tools you need—energy, oxygen, muscle power, fuel, pain resistance, and mental acuity—all at a moment's notice.

> *Stress can have many positive effects such as challenging us to perform at higher levels, motivating us, keeping us at our peak, and focusing our thoughts and behaviors to reach an important goal or objective.*

Here is an example of how this works:

Stressor: You are a customer service representative. Your company puts a lot of pressure on you to "up sell" more products to customers who call in for problems with their system. Your boss informs you that you are below quota and in danger, even though your customers seem extremely appreciative of the help you have been giving them.

What Happens in Your Brain if You Perceive This as Stress:

(1) Immediately stress hormones are released into your body, the primary one being *cortisol*. Cortisol is very important in marshaling systems throughout your body (including the heart, lungs, circulation, metabolism, immune system, and skin) to deal quickly with your boss.

(2) Other chemical messengers known as "catecholamines" are released. The most well-known of these is "adrenaline." These messengers activate an area inside the brain called the "amygdala" which is thought to trigger your emotional response to your boss's threats. Common emotional reactions would be fear of losing your job, anger at the pressure, etc.

(3) Chemical messages are also sent to another brain structure called the "hippocampus" to store your emotional experience with your boss into a long-term memory. Thus, your brain will alert you to "danger" in similar future situations.

Response by your heart, lungs, and circulation:

If you continue to experience your boss's remarks as an acute stress, your body will continue to try to respond to it in these ways:

(1) Your breathing becomes rapid as your lungs try to take in more oxygen.

(2) Your blood flow may actually increase 300%-400%, priming the muscles, lungs, and brain for added demands. Your stress system thinks you are going to either fight your boss or run away, so it is preparing your body for either outcome.

(3) Your spleen discharges red and white blood cells (who knew?) allowing your blood to transport more oxygen.

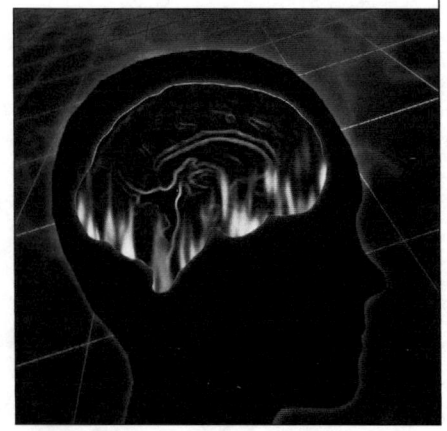

Warning signs that you may be stressed out:

- Feeling depressed, edgy, guilty, tired

- Having headaches or stomachaches

- Trouble sleeping or eating

- Laughing or crying for no reason

- Blaming other people for bad things that happen to you

- Only seeing the down side of a situation

- Feeling like things that you used to enjoy aren't fun or are a burden

- Resenting other people or your responsibilities

- Muscle tension

Your Immune System's response:

At this point, your body sees your boss as an enemy and thinks it has to line up defensive soldiers to deal with the threat in case you get injured.

(1) Your released hormones dampen parts of your immune system, so that infection fighters (including important white blood cells) can be redistributed.

(2) These immune-boosting troops are sent to your body's front lines where injury or infection is most likely, such as the skin, bone marrow and the lymph nodes. After all, who knows where the boss will strike?

That Dry Mouth

The more you think about what your boss said, the more stressed you become. What if you lose your job? What will your husband say? How will you pay the bills? How can I satisfy both my boss and my customers?

As your stress response continues, fluids are diverted from nonessential locations, including your mouth. This causes dryness and difficulty in talking which is a problem if you are a customer service representative. In addition, since stress can cause spasms in your throat muscles, you may have trouble swallowing.

Talk About a Bad Hair Day...

Your stress response diverts blood flow away from the skin to support the heart and muscle tissues. (This also reduces blood loss in the event your boss hits you). The physical effect is a cool, clammy, sweaty skin. The scalp also tightens so that your hair seems to stand up.

Four Steps to Stress Management

Step 1
Develop Stress Alert!

Step 2
Make Life Changes

Step 3
Adjust Mind-View

Step 4
Apply Stress-Guard

Four Steps to Stress Management

Step 1 – Stress-Alert!

This means becoming aware that you are stressed out.
Many people simply are not aware of how stressed out they actually are, or how stress may be affecting their health and their behavior. Learning to recognize the signs is the first step toward dealing with your stress.

What signs do you notice before becoming stressed out?

Sign #1 _____

_____

Sign #2 _____

_____

Sign #3 _____

_____

Sign #4 _____

Step 2 – Make Life Changes to Reduce Your Stress Triggers

Some stresses in your life are changeable, but it takes effort and commitment to make those necessary life changes. The most common stresses in this category are related to how you manage time, how you manage finances, how you deal with family and relationships, and the amount of "overload" you have in your daily life. Another changeable stress is the "match" between you and your job or occupation.

Eight Practical Tips for Reducing Stress Triggers:

(1) *Take time off* – Take a vacation or a long weekend. During the work day, take a short break to stretch. Walk, breathe slowly, take a day off and go to the beach, and relax.

(2) *Manage your time* – Set realistic goals and deadlines. Plan projects accordingly. Do "must do" tasks first. Schedule difficult tasks for the time of day when you are most productive. Tackle easy tasks when you feel low on energy or motivation.

www.centuryangermanagement.com / Copyright 2005

> *Some stresses in your life are changeable, but it takes effort and commitment to make those necessary life changes.*

(3) **Set limits** – When necessary, learn to say "no" in a friendly but firm manner.

(4) **Choose your battles wisely** – Don't rush to argue every time someone disagrees with you. Keep a cool head and avoid pointless arguments altogether.

(5) **Use calming skills** – Learn not to act on your first impulse. Give your anger time to subside. Anger needs to be expressed, but it is often wise to do something that takes your mind off the situation. The break allows you to compose yourself and respond to the anger in a more effective manner.

(6) **If appropriate, look for less stressful job options** – But first, ask yourself whether you have given your job a fair chance.

(7) **Take control of what you can** – For example, if you're working too many hours and you can't study enough, ask your boss if you can cut back.

(8) **Don't commit yourself to things you can't or don't want to do** – If you're already too busy, don't promise to decorate for the school dance. If you're tired and don't want to go out, tell your friends you'll go out another night. Learn to take care of yourself.

What are the main sources of stress in your life and how could you reduce them?

☐ Financial _____

_____

_____

☐ Relationship _____

_____

_____

☐ Family _____

_____

_____

_____

> **Many of the stress triggers in our lives don't need to stress us out if we just change our perspective on them or develop better resources to deal with them.**

☐ Work _____

_____

_____

☐ Time _____

_____

_____

☐ Overload _____

_____

_____

Step 3 – Adjust Your Mind-View

For a potential stress trigger to stress us out and affect us, it first has to be experienced or perceived as a stressor.

Here is an example:

Imagine, if you will, that there is a lion on the other side of that closed door you see at the other end of this room. If I can convince you there is a lion there, and you hear the growling, smell the lion, and hear the scratching at the door, how are you going to respond?

Usual response: *"I would be afraid and try to figure out how to get out of here."*

And what would your body be doing?

Usual Response: *"My heart would be racing, my muscles would tense, I would be focused on escaping."*

Now, consider the following: In terms of your stress reaction to this scenario, does it really make any difference if the lion is really there or not?

What causes the stress reaction in you is:

(1) **Your *perception or belief* that the lion is there** – not the reality of the lion being there or not!

> *You can change your mind-set towards many things in your life that will reduce your stress. Start by changing the conversation you have with yourself*

(2) **Your *memory* of danger in a similar situation.** Now, I know that you may never have encountered a lion at your door before, but you certainly have had experiences with the unknown, or wild animals, or seen ferocious lions at a circus or at the zoo.

(3) **An *emotional reaction* to the event, usually fear.** The extent of this emotional reaction will be determined in part on how unpleasant or traumatic the original event was that you are remembering.

Many of the stress triggers in our lives don't need to stress us out if we just change our perspective on them or develop better resources to deal with them. For instance, if you developed the skills of a lion tamer, that lion out there wouldn't bother you at all!

Likewise, you can change your mind-set toward many things in your life that will reduce your stress. Start by changing the conversation you have with yourself by trying the following self-statements to reduce your stress:

- Don't sweat the small stuff. And remember: It's all *small* stuff.

- I can deal with this; I have dealt with much more stress in the past.

- Will this be important five years from now or even next month?

- This does not have to be catastrophic; it is merely a blip in my existence.

- Tough times never last; tough people do.

- My anger is a signal. Time to talk to myself and to relax.

- It is impossible to control other people and situations. The ONLY thing I can control is myself and how I express my feelings.

- If people criticize me, I can survive that. Nothing says that I have to be perfect.

- Sometimes the things that stress me are stupid and insignificant. I can recognize that my feelings come from having old primary feelings restimulated. It is OK to walk away from the conflict or problem.

- I am feeling stressed because I don't have the resources to deal with this situation right now; I don't need to berate myself or put myself down over it.

Applying this principal to your life, how could you reduce stress by having a different mind-view about a stressor?

_____

_____

_____

_____

_____

_____

_____

_____

_____

_____

> *Let's face it, some stressors are unavoidable and are a part of our lives— at least for the time being. In this case, we should learn ways to lessen the effects of stress in order to minimize the damage.*

Step 4 – Apply Stress-Guard

Let's face it, some stressors are unavoidable and are a part of our lives —at least for the time being. In this case, we should learn ways to lessen the effects of stress in order to minimize the damage. Stress-guards include improving your health through diet and exercise, relaxation or meditation techniques, sleeping better, and developing social support networks.

Exercise

We all know that exercise is good for us; its effect on stress and your health is considerable. For example, numerous studies have shown that simple walking is one of the best ways to prevent heart disease. Some of the most promising research has to do with the way exercise affects the brain. Running, for instance, appears to make humans smarter (now, isn't that a great stress-reducer?) Other aerobic activities such as jogging, swimming, biking, etc. for twenty minutes three times per week is helpful in reducing stress.

www.centuryangermanagement.com / Copyright 2005

> *The ability to recognize how your body reacts to stressors in your life can be a powerful skill. Most people are more aware of the weather, the time of day, or their bank balance than they are of the tension in their own bodies.*

Diet

A healthy diet helps to stress-guard us in many ways. According to some scientists, when you feel threatened or pressured for a period of time, your body assumes that energy supplies are being drained. Your stress response kicks in automatically, not distinguishing between running away from a predator and getting ready to fight with your spouse.

As part of this process, your liver is signaled to convert energy into long-term storage. Your stress hormones then encourage food-seeking behavior, making sure that your supplies are replenished. In one of biology's ironies, stress makes us hungry. If we then make poor food choices, our stress responses are intensified in ways that can very quickly spin out of control.

It is also important to avoid caffeine and to not cope with stress by using alcohol or drugs. If you are stressed out, caffeine is like throwing gasoline on a fire to put it out!

Sleep

Scientists know that sleep is a vitally important activity in the natural world, although the exact reasons for this are not yet known. Sleep deprivation qualifies as a stressor in the sense of making life miserable and in the sense of producing more "load" on us to cope with. Trying to maintain normal sleep/wake patterns can greatly aid our ability to cope with our world when we are awake.

Relaxation/Meditation

Much research shows that relaxation or meditation can greatly reduce our stress and put us into a "health envelope." Studies show you should meditate twice a day for 20 minutes to achieve this result. But, you can also learn to meditate at work or standing in line at the grocery store. The trick is to breath deeply and then to focus on your here-and-now body feelings, putting distracting thoughts out of your mind. It is amazing what even a two minute exercise can do to reduce your stress and make you feel better.

The ability to recognize how your body reacts to stressors in your life can be a powerful skill. Most people are more aware of the weather, the time of day, or their bank balance than they are of the tension in their own bodies.

Your body registers stress long before your conscious mind does. Muscle tension is your body's way of letting you know that you are under stress. Body awareness is the first step toward acknowledging and reducing stress.

Breathing exercises have been found to be effective in reducing stress as well as anxiety disorders, panic attacks, depression, muscle tension, irritability, headaches, and fatigue.

> *Your body registers stress long before your conscious mind does... Body awareness is the first step toward acknowledging and reducing stress.*

The following exercise can be used at work or at home:

Counting Breaths

(1) Sit or lie down in a comfortable position with your arms and legs uncrossed and your spine straight.

(2) Breath in deeply into your abdomen. Let yourself pause before you exhale.

(3) As you exhale, count "One" to yourself. As you continue to inhale and exhale, count each exhalation by saying "Two, three, four."

(4) Continue counting your exhalations in sets of four for five to ten minutes.

(5) Notice your breathing gradually slowing, your body relaxing, and your mind calming as you practice this breathing mediation.

Another great breathing exercise is the following; give it a try and notice the effects:

Letting Go of Tension

(1) Sit comfortably in a chair with your feet on the floor.

(2) Breathe deeply into your abdomen and say to yourself, "Breathe in relaxation." Let yourself pause before you exhale.

(3) Breathe out from your abdomen and say to yourself, "Breathe out tension." Pause before you inhale.

(4) Use each inhalation as a moment to become aware of any tension in your body.

(5) Use each exhalation as an opportunity to let go of tension.

(6) You may find it helpful to use your imagination to picture or feel the relaxation entering and the tension leaving your body.

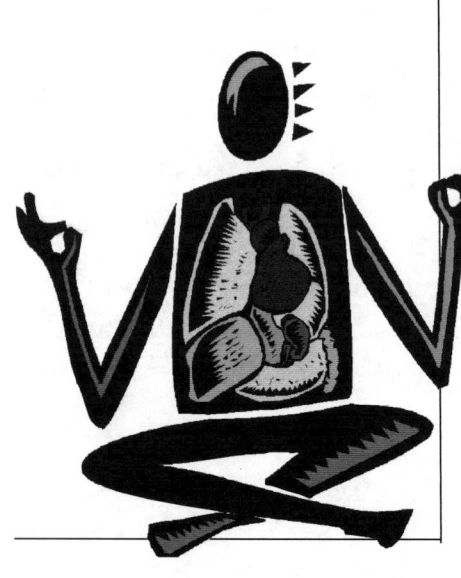

www.centuryangermanagement.com / Copyright 2005

Social Support

Talking to your family or friends can help by giving you a chance to express your feelings. But problems in your social life or family can be the hardest to talk about. If you think you can't talk to your family or a friend, look for someone outside the situation like your priest or minister, a counselor, or your family doctor.

On the other side of the coin, protect yourself from negative coworkers, relationships, or family members. Do not get caught up in others' negative thinking. They will only serve to rip off your peace of mind and positive energy. Take good care of yourself and learn to recognize whether a person will help you or hinder you. Include in your inner circle only positive and encouraging people, who will hold you accountable to your new goals.

How do you need to stress-guard your life?

☐ More Exercise: *Plan* _____

_____

_____

_____

_____

_____

_____

☐ Better Diet: *Plan* _____

_____

_____

_____

_____

_____

_____

_____

> *Include in your inner circle only positive and encouraging people who will hold you accountable to your new goals.*

☐ Relaxation/Meditation: *Plan* _____

_____

_____

_____

_____

_____

_____

_____

☐ Social Support: *Plan* _____

_____

_____

_____

_____

_____

_____

_____

> **Positive attitudes really help. Choose to see difficulties as opportunities for growth.**

Ten Tips to Reduce Stress

Tip #1

Take 40 deep slow breaths each day. Spread them evenly throughout your day to avoid hyperventilating. You can benefit from associating the deep breaths with some common work occurrence such as the telephone ringing or watching the clock.

Tip #2

Use regular relaxation periods for work breaks. Try fifteen to twenty minute periods of undisturbed time away from the phone and/or family. Commit to using this for four to six weeks to begin to see the benefits. Suggestion: Take a short walk.

www.centuryangermanagement.com / Copyright 2005

> *Remember that you cannot control all the people and situations that happen around you. The only one you can truly control is yourself and the way you respond to stressful people and situations.*

Tip #3

Get regular exercise. Aerobic activities such as walking, jogging, swimming, biking, etc. for 20 minutes 3 times per week is helpful in reducing stress. It kicks off stress-reducing chemicals in your brain. Be sure to check with your doctor first if you have any health issues.

Tip #4

Eat sensibly. Avoid caffeine. Do not cope with stress by using alcohol or drugs. If you are stressed out, caffeine is like throwing gasoline on a fire to put it out!

Tip #5

Plan for growth in all aspects of your life, not just work and finance (i.e. family, relationships, spiritual interests, vacations, hobbies, etc.). At the end of your life, you will not wish that you had spent more time at the office or that you had made more money.

Tip #6

Positive attitudes really help. Choose to see difficulties as opportunities for growth.

Tip #7

Protect yourself from negative coworkers and relationships. Do not get caught up in others' negative thinking. They will only serve to rip off your peace of mind and positive energy. Take good care of yourself. Learn to recognize whether a person will help you or hinder you. Include in your inner circle only positive and encouraging people who will hold you accountable to your new goals.

Tip #8

Remember that you cannot control all the people and situations that happen around you. The only one you can truly control is yourself and the way you respond to stressful people and situations.

Tip #9

Give sincere compliments freely and smile. Choose to look for the good things happening around you every day; you might be surprised at what you will find.

Tip #10

Learn to really listen. It is the best communication technique that you can develop. It is the highest act of love that a person can do for another.

NOTES

Anger Control Tool #2
Empathy

> *Our ability to know how we are feeling as well our ability to accurately sense the feelings of those around us help to make positive connections with others*

Emotions and Our Lives

Have you ever been in a restaurant and noticed that the customers at the table next to you were speaking louder than anyone else? It was as if they had no idea that they were being so loud and intrusive to the rest of the patrons. This lack of awareness is often a sign of not being emotionally or socially alert. Or, have you ever been in a situation in which you tried to express your feelings and it backfired in some way? It is hard sometimes to express our emotions.

The expression of emotion is often passed down from our parents, guardians or caregivers as children. Many of us often express our emotions, or lack the ability to do so, based on what we learned in childhood. Some of us are very good at knowing how we feel and expressing it, while others struggle to do so. It is crucial to express emotion in order to relate to those around us. Our ability to know how we are feeling as well as our ability to accurately sense the feelings of those around us help to make positive connections with others. This characteristic is often called "empathy."

Emotions are what allow us to grow in love. Emotions are also the stuff of poetry, art, and music. Emotions fill us with a sense of connection to others. In many ways, emotions make life worth living. How we experience the world, relate to others, and find meaning in life are dependent upon how we regulate our emotions.

People who have the ability to understand and regulate their emotions as well as sense and understand the emotions of others are said to have a quality called "emotional intelligence" (EQ), a new term coined by psychologists. Research shows that persons with high "EQ" excel in leadership, sales, academic performance, marriage, friendships and overall health. Two of the most important traits associated with emotional intelligence are empathy, and social awareness.

Why Empathy is Important

Nature developed our emotions over millions of years of evolution and they serve an important social function. This function is that of allowing one person to have a sense of the mental state of another person. Empathy is the capacity to feel another person's experience.

As one English author wrote: *"To empathize is to see with the eyes of another, to hear with the ears of another, to feel with the heart of another."*

Empathy requires knowing the perspective of others and being able to see things from the value and belief system of the other person. It is the ability to fully immerse oneself in another's viewpoint, yet be able to remain wholly apart.

Empathy is important in the world because lack of it leads to poor communication and a failure to understand others. Empathy on a personal level is important because it allows us to understand social interactions and anticipate the behavior of others. Empathy also allows others to understand us; when we are with highly empathetic people, we feel *felt* by the other – that is, that they are emotionally attuned to us and can see the world from our point of view.

Lack of Empathy

Lack of empathy leads to all sorts of problems in our world. Nations go to war, people get killed, couples divorce – all for a lack of empathy and understanding. Our prisons are filled with people who don't have the capacity to feel their victim's pain or suffering. This lack of empathy keeps them from feeling what it is like to be hurt.

A lack of empathy is a sign that people think only of themselves. These people are concerned only with their own ideas and feelings – not others'. They push only their own issues while not seeing the needs of others.

> *Empathy on a personal level is important because it allows us to understand social interactions and anticipate the behavior of others.*

> *Some people seem to go through life almost oblivious to the impact they are having on others in their world.*

Why Social Awareness is Important

Some people seem to go through life almost oblivious to the impact they are having on others in their world. Often they upset people at work or in their family due to their behavior, but seem stunned when they find out that people are reacting to them in a negative way. Lacking empathy, they aren't able to "read" others enough to see what impact their behavior is having, so they keep on doing the same thing —which unfortunately keeps getting them the same result.

One way to increase awareness is to operate on two levels in your mind at the same time; in computer language, it is like running the main program, but also having another program running silently in the background. The main program is what you are trying to communicate (for instance, "you need to complete that project before you go home tonight"). The other program is imagining how you look or sound to the other person while you are delivering the main message.

Many anger management participants find the following technique extremely useful. When talking to someone, imagine there is video camera in the corner of the room recording your behavior. Ask yourself:

• How am I looking right now?

• How am I being seen from the viewpoint of other people?

• Is the message I'm delivering the same one as they are receiving?

How Can You Learn to be More Empathetic?

The feeling of empathy starts at a very young age and probably is developed by the manner in which infant and parent are attached to each other emotionally. This attachment is formed by parents or caretakers responding to the infant's feelings in a positive way so that the infant learns to trust and to be concerned with the feelings of other people. Babies with secure attachment to their parents have a head start on less fortunate babies who have parents that produce insecurity or uncertainty in their children.

From birth, a baby can become upset when it hears another baby crying; this may be the groundwork for later empathy. Studies show that babies as young as nine months old can be aware of other babies' pain and suffering—definitely a sign of empathy.

Empathy is built through increased awareness of yourself. The more

you understand yourself, and your emotions, the better you will be in understanding, appreciating, and relating to the feelings of others. As you develop empathic ability, you will find it more and more difficult to stay angry at people.

> *Empathic listening is much more than just hearing. It is listening while you suspend your normal "filters" that determine what you hear.*

Empathic Listening

Empathic listening is a type of listening that goes further than ordinary listening. This type of listening uses another person's point of view to see the world as others see it. It provides a higher level of understanding of how others feel.

Empathic listening is not a skill that most people have, but it can be developed with practice. Empathic listening is much more than just hearing. It is listening while you suspend your normal "filters" that determine what you hear. Everyone has these filters; if your filter is different from another's, you may "hear" the exact same message in a different way than he or she does.

What are some common filters that influence what we hear?

Filter 1 – "The right/wrong" filter
Using this, you listen for evidence that what the other person is saying is wrong and you are right. If you are indeed listening to justify your position, you can hardly be listening with empathy.

Filter 2 – "Loved/not loved" filter
With this, we completely miss the point of what our companion might be trying to communicate to us, because all we are listening for is "do they still love me?" or "are they going to leave me?"

Filter 3 – "Criticism/put-down" filter
Any complaint or problem the other person has is heard as a personal put-down or criticism of us, rather than a legitimate complaint the other person may have. For example, your partner says, "I can't stand living in this neighborhood anymore." What you hear is: "If I made more money and I was more adequate as a person, she wouldn't be upset with me."

Filter 4 – "What am I going to say next?" filter
This is listening, but with your answer running. Your real goal with this type of listening is to "one-up" the other, to prepare a comeback, to have a better story, to promote your self-interest, or to prove someone wrong.

Are you a good listener?

Listening Skill:

Try to understand the other person's point of view

- ☐ **Yes**
- ☐ **No**
- ☐ **Maybe**

Fail to hear what is said because you are thinking about what to say?

- ☐ **Yes**
- ☐ **No**
- ☐ **Maybe**

Think of yourself as the other person talks?

- ☐ **Yes**
- ☐ **No**
- ☐ **Maybe**

Drift in and out of the conversation, instead of listening intently?

- ☐ **Yes**
- ☐ **No**
- ☐ **Maybe**

Becoming impatient with the other person while they are trying to explain something

- ☐ **Yes**
- ☐ **No**
- ☐ **Maybe**

Clearly communicate to the other person that you are listening?

- ☐ **Yes**
- ☐ **No**
- ☐ **Maybe**

Filter 5 – "Get to the point" filter

Maybe you've noticed that some people's conversations are like a bullet train—direct and to the destination—while others' are like a long trip down the Amazon River, taking in all the tributaries and scenery. If you only listen in order to "get to the point," you might miss important information that will help you understand how the other person experiences his or her world. Persons who use this filter are often very impatient.

Empathic listening leads to a better understanding of people and fewer mistakes and misunderstandings in almost all situations. It is a start to solving numerous problems with our family members as well as co-workers. Good listening is a valuable tool to build trust with others and win respect, qualities needed to be seen as a leader and to be successful.

Communication

Empathic communication requires awareness of the messages you are sending and the messages you are receiving from the other person. Some of the messages are delivered or received with words while the majority of the messages (probably 80%) are done with nonverbal communication.

Let's start with the words and phrases we use to communicate. Avoid barriers to effective communication because they make it difficult for you to listen to others with empathy or have others listen to you in an empathetic manner:

Barriers to Effective Communication

(1) **Commanding** phrases like, *"You must…"* or *"You have to…"*

(2) **Browbeating** phrases like, *"If you don't, then…"* or *"You better or else…"*

(3) **"Shoulding" people** phrases like, *"It is your duty to…,"* *"You should…,"* or *"You ought to…"*

(4) **Scolding** phrases like, *"Let me tell you why you are wrong…,"* or *"Do you realize…"*

(5) **Giving unrequested advice** like, *"What I would do is…"* or *"It would be best if you…"*

(6) **Morally judgmental** phrases like, *"You are bad/lazy"* that make a person feel like their character is being judged.

(7) **Playing shrink** like, *"You're just trying to get attention..."* or *"I know what you need..."*

(8) **Being a district attorney** with many irritating questions such as *"Why? What? How? When? Who?"* and other prying types of questions.

In addition to avoiding these known barriers to empathic communication, you should also be aware of your nonverbal messages such as:

- **Facial expressions** - The language of our emotions is spoken by our faces — Not with the words that come out of our mouths but with expressions formed by our facial muscles. Researchers have found that 43 muscles create 10,000 visible facial configurations of which 3000 are meaningful in terms of expressing emotion.

  These emotional expressions are universal and do not depend on any particular learning or culture that we are in. This means that people around the world basically have the same expressions in their faces revealing their emotions and these emotions can be read accurately by people in different parts of the world from very diverse cultures. This fact can help unite people because emotional expression serves as a common thread among all human beings.

- **Touch** is a very basic way to connect with other human beings which, like facial expressions, is a natural form of communication that everyone understands. Touch can be a powerful, trusted way to communicate both your feelings and also that you understand how someone else feels. The right touch at the right time can say mountains – even though it may last only a moment.

- **Eye gaze/ contact** is an important communication tool in learning to feel empathy for another human being. It has been said that the eyes are the window to the soul. Eye contact helps you feel "connected" to others and also helps others feel connected to you. Eye contact means different things in different cultures, however; it is not quite the "universal" language that touch and facial expressions are.

- **Tone of Voice** refers to the manner in which a verbal statement is presented, e.g., its rhythm, breathiness, hoarseness, or loudness. Your tone of voice reflects emotion and mood. It may also carry social information, as in a sarcastic, superior, or submissive manner

> *If your words and tone are not in agreement, you can bet that the listener will be responding to your tone as much or more as to your words.*

Empathy Quiz

Skill:

Empathic Listening
- ☐ **Have**
- ☐ **Maybe**
- ☐ **Need to Develop**

Acceptance
- ☐ **Have**
- ☐ **Maybe**
- ☐ **Need to Develop**

Non-Judgment
- ☐ **Have**
- ☐ **Maybe**
- ☐ **Need to Develop**

Avoid Roadblocks
to Communication
- ☐ **Have**
- ☐ **Maybe**
- ☐ **Need to Develop**

> *We must allow people to have feelings without telling them how they should feel or think.*

of speaking.

Many voice qualities are universal across all human cultures (though they are also subject to cultural modification and shaping). For instance, adults use higher pitched voices to speak to infants and young children. The softer pitch is innately "friendly" and suggests a nonaggressive, nonhostile pose. With each other, men and women use higher pitched voices in greetings and in courtship to show harmlessness and to invite physical closeness.

To increase empathy, it is extremely important to be mindful of the message being conveyed by the tone of voice of another. When relating to others, be especially aware of your tone and ask yourself if it is consistent with the words you are using. If your words and tone are not in agreement, you can bet that the listener will be responding to your tone as much or more as to your words.

- **Stance and physical appearance** communicate to us much about how a person is feeling and also gives others non-verbal messages regarding our emotional states. How close someone stands to us, for instance, may be a message as to their positive feelings for us. Folded arms may signal defensiveness; clenched hands on hips with outstretched elbows and a legs-apart stance is typical of mothers scolding their children and may remind us of being scolded.

Acceptance

Acceptance is the ability to see that others have a right to their feelings and viewpoints. We must allow people to have feelings without telling them how they should feel or think. Acceptance of others' feelings is not easy when people act differently than we do. Empathetic people understand that feelings are difficult to control and that most people do the best they can at the time with the knowledge, skills, abilities, or information that have.

Try not to judge others, even though it is common to have difficulty with those who are different from us. Remember that had your life circumstances been exactly like those of another, you may have made the same decisions. As someone very wise once said, "Do not judge another until you have walked a mile in his or her shoes."

To practice acceptance as an empathy skill it is also important to keep in mind that people have limitations and unique vulnerabilities. Understanding this and being more tolerant of others with their limitations is a major step toward empathy.

Notes

_____

_____

_____

_____

_____

_____

_____

_____

_____

_____

_____

_____

_____

_____

_____

_____

_____

_____

_____

_____

_____

_____

Anger Control Tool #3
Respond Instead of React

> *Insanity: doing the same thing over and over again and expecting different results.*
> **–John Dryden**
> (English Poet)

When you go to the doctor's office and he taps you below your kneecap with his little hammer, what happens? In most cases, your leg extends automatically. This happens involuntarily—you do not consciously think, "I will extend my leg when the doctor taps my knee."

In a similar manner, while driving when you come to a stop sign, you usually apply your brakes and stop without thinking much about it—in fact, you may be listening to something on the radio, or talking to your children while stopping. You have developed a "habit," an automatic reaction of applying brakes when coming to a stop sign.

What about your emotions? Do we have a choice as to how we will deal with the emotions felt when confronted with people or situations that trigger certain feelings in us?

The answer to that question is a little bit complicated and all scientists, researchers, and doctors do not yet agree on the answer. Most would agree however, that one of the unique characteristics of human beings, as opposed to other animals, is the ability to have *choices* in how we deal with things that happen to us—even if the emotions that are triggered in us are not 100% under our control when they first occur. There are those who say that only two things in life are absolutes—death and taxes. Everything else is a choice. What do you think?

Let's look at an example. If a driver cuts you off on the freeway, a common emotion to feel is frustration and anger. Is this under your

> *Having choices means that we can make decisions about how we will respond to a situation.*

control? Maybe not immediately. It would be quite natural to instantly and automatically feel those emotions to some extent (although even this would vary a lot from person to person or situation to situation). But, *what would be* under your control is how frustrated or angry you get, how long these feelings last, what you do with these feelings, and how you behave while having these feelings. And, that control comes from knowing you have choices.

Having choices means that we can make *decisions* about how we will respond to a situation—rather than just reacting to it like our leg does to the doctor's examination. This involves taking personal responsibility for your feelings and your behavior. To easily remember this idea, instead of saying the word *"responsible,"* say *"response-able."*

Some people just have a really hard time understanding this concept of being "response-able," as they go through life constantly blaming others and circumstances for their anger and angry behavior. As an example, we recently had a phone call from a woman inquiring about our anger management classes who asked what was taught in the program. We explained the eight tools of anger control to her, after which she said "What? You mean I'm the one that has to do the changing?"

Flexibility is Sign of Good Mental Health

Yes, we told her, anger management works much better when people accept the idea of personal responsibility for their feelings and their behavior. In fact, being "flexible" in how we respond to a situation is one of the signs of good mental health. Persons with flexibility do not continue to do the things that get results they don't want. Instead, they are able to adjust—or fine tune— their responses depending on the situation and the outcome they desire.

There are many advantages to learning to be more flexible—and "response-able"—in dealing with the stresses and frustrations of your life. At the top of the list is a sense of empowerment. It just feels good and powerful to know that you are in charge of your response, rather than being controlled by other people or circumstances. Many people notice their anger level going down as their feeling of empowerment goes up.

Another advantage to being more flexible in your responses is that it changes how people respond to you. This is a great way to reduce conflict in your life and change the rules of how others treat you — without having to get angry, demanding, or aggressive. Let's look at some common examples to illustrate how more flexibility in

responding can remarkably change your emotions and your life:

Example 1: *Breanna, a 32 year old married woman, shared in an anger management class that her relationship with her ex-husband had changed drastically once she applied this tool of "respond instead of react." Where previously she would instantly get enraged when her ex threatened to file for custody of their two small children, she now bit her tongue, and simply remained quiet when he began threatening an escalated legal battle. Unable to get the usual reaction from her, he calmed down and instantly became rational and more reasonable.*

Example 2: *Tom, a 42-year old owner of an insurance agency, could not keep office staff working for him due to what was seen as constant anger, irritability, and rudeness toward them. Being a high-energy person, he was constantly in motion, making demands on his staff that antagonized everybody in his office. In anger management class, we taught him simply to be more polite in his approach to others. This included responding in a nicer way and with more respect for the dignity and value of his employees. Amazingly, this resulted in staff "seeing him" in a different light which then led to their behaving quite differently toward him. As an added benefit, productivity increased noticeably once employees felt valued and no longer spent so much time being angry with their boss.*

Example 3: *28-year old Tom was a real estate appraiser who spent a great deal of time on Southern California freeways, traveling from appointment to appointment. He was constantly frustrated, however, due to the aggressive drivers he encountered on a daily basis, cutting in front of him, changing lanes, and generally being inconsiderate. He began reacting with aggression himself, resulting in an escalating "dance" to the point that someone actually followed him off an exit and confronted him. At this point, Tom realized he needed to respond differently to aggressive drivers. So, he changed his driving behavior—being more considerate, staying safe distances behind others, allowing others more lane changes, etc. He also began listening to opera during his traveling, which calmed him considerably. He was astounded to discover that somehow he was encountering fewer aggressive drivers after he himself changed.*

Three Ways to Respond Differently

Many of our anger students tell us they want to respond differently and be more flexible in dealing with life's stresses and anger triggers, but they feel overwhelmed because they don't know how to do it, or where to start. The answer is to see it as a three-step process:

Step 1 - Look at your attitude

Step 2 - Find ways to regulate your emotions

> **It just feels good and powerful to know that you are in charge of your response, rather than being controlled by other people or circumstances.**

Jerry's Story

Jerry is the manager of a restaurant in America. He is always in a good mood and always has something positive to say. When someone would ask him how he was doing, he would always reply, "If I were any better, I would be twins!"

Many of the waiters at his restaurant quit their jobs when he changed jobs, so they could follow him around from restaurant to restaurant. The reason the waiters followed Jerry was because of his attitude.

He was a natural motivator. If an employee was having a bad day, Jerry was always there, telling the employee how to look on the positive side of the situation.

Jerry's attitude: "Each morning I wake up and say to myself, I have two choices today. I can choose to be in a good mood or I can choose to be in a bad mood. I always choose to be in a good mood.

Each time something bad happens, I can choose to be a victim or I can choose to learn from it. I always choose to learn. Life is all about choices.

When you cut away all the junk, every situation is a choice. You choose how you react to situations. You choose how people will affect your mood. You choose to be in a good mood or bad mood."

Several years later, Jerry accidentally did something you are never supposed to do in the restaurant business: he left the back door of his restaurant open one morning and was robbed by three armed men. While trying to open the safe, his hand, shaking from nervousness slipped off the combination.

Continued on the following page >

Step 3 - Try alternative behaviors

Step 1– Look At Your Attitude

As we have discussed in several places in this book, our attitude toward what happens to us can drastically alter our feelings toward it. Nothing illustrates this better than Jerry's story, (see left column), provided to us by one of our anger management class graduates.

That negative voice in your head can be quite convincing —persuading you to judge others, be pessimistic, or think negatively, all the while pulling in all the destructive feelings that go along with those destructive thoughts. As Jerry illustrates in his story, you can create a louder, more persuasive voice that helps you find an equally believable, more optimistic viewpoint. You'll be more likely to cut others some slack, cut yourself more slack, see more options, and feel less angry!

Attitude change can also help you *appreciate* more what's right in your world and in your life, and that can help you regulate your feelings. Research scientists at the Institute for HeartMath have discovered that generating feelings of gratitude, on purpose, reduces the amount of damaging stress hormones in your body. Also, adopting a habit of appreciation sets up a positive self-fulfilling prophecy— since you are in the practice of identifying things to appreciate, you are more likely to notice those things.

Step 2 – Regulate Your Emotions

To understand this concept we need to look inside our heads for a moment, in that part of our brain called the limbic system that is where most of our emotions live. While the amount of flexibility we have in our emotions is dependent on many things including our genes, our emotional experiences early in life, and our stress levels, new research is showing that our brains are very plastic and to some extent can be molded throughout our lives. In fact, scientists now believe that the everyday experiences we have can actually change our brain structure and brain chemistry. No longer is it thought that all those connections in our brain that determine our feelings and behavior are fixed for life after a certain age.

What this means for people learning to manage anger better is that by learning to respond differently to all those anger "triggers" in your life may actually be a way to modify how your brain is wired—so that it may be easier to deal with future anger triggers. You may still get angry,

The robbers panicked and shot him. Luckily, Jerry was found quickly and rushed to the hospital. After 18 hours of surgery and weeks of intensive care, Jerry was released from the hospital with fragments of the bullets still in his body.

Ask to describe what happened, he said: "The first thing that went through my mind was that I should have locked the back door."

"Then, after they shot me, as I lay on the floor, remembered that I had two choices: I could choose to live or choose to die. I chose to live."

When they wheeled me into the Emergency Room and I saw the expressions on the faces of the doctors and nurses, I got really scared. In their eyes, I read 'He's a dead man.' I knew I needed to take action."

"There was a big nurse shouting questions at me," said Jerry. "She asked if I was allergic to anything."

Yes,' I replied. The doctors and nurses stopped working as they waited for my reply. I took a deep breath and yelled, 'Bullets!' Over their laughter, I told them, 'I am choosing to live. Please operate on me as if I am alive, not dead'."

Jerry lived thanks to the skill of his doctors, but also because of his amazing attitude. We learn from him that EVERY DAY YOU HAVE THE CHOICE TO EITHER ENJOY YOUR LIFE, OR TO HATE IT.

The only thing that is truly yours that no one can control or take from you - is YOUR ATTITUDE, so if you can take care of that, everything else in life becomes much easier. ■

—**Author Unknown**

but less so as your brain responds differently to new information and life experiences.

New research in neuroscience is showing that your brain is constantly searching for signals from your body about what is going on inside, and then creates emotions based on that information. Our awareness of bodily states, such as tension in our muscles, shifts in our facial expressions, or signals from our heart or intestines, lets us know how we feel through bodily feedback.

This exciting finding gives us more tools to regulate our emotions, and thus manage many of our feelings, including anger. For example, if you contract facial muscles in a frown, you are more likely to enter a negative state of mind. On the other hand, if we sense our own faces smiling, we are more likely to enter a positive state of mind and to view what is going on in our lives more positively.

There are many other ways to regulate our emotions and our feelings in response to frustrating, irritating, or disappointing people or situations in our lives. For instance, Dr. David Burns, who wrote the book *Feeling Good*, suggests being your own best friend. This means thinking of the advice you gave a dear friend in a difficult time and take that advice yourself! Eat well, exercise, relax, play, and avoid cigarettes and alcohol. These practices set up the conditions in your life that will make it easier to regulate your emotions.

Other suggestions for emotional regulation that have helped many people struggling with anger, stress, or depression include: listening to the type of music that alters your mood in a positive way; getting in touch with a spiritual system that centers or balances you and brings you comfort; and creating emotional connections with others by sincere listening (research shows that when you are completely attentive to what someone else is saying, your blood pressure drops).

Step 3 – Try Alternative Behaviors

Behaving differently is one of the most effective ways to show response flexibility and get different results in your life. But, doing things differently is not easy because we are creatures of habit and we tend to behave in ways that we are familiar and comfortable with. While it often feels risky or uncomfortable to try different approaches to deal with things that make us angry, it is worth the effort because, as the saying goes, "If you keep doing what you do, you will keep getting what you've got."

One of the challenges in behaving differently is, of course, coming up with ideas about other ways we can behave in a situation. There is a strong tendency to repeat our past and do things as we have learned to do them—often starting in our childhood—without questioning or challenging what we do.

Take, for instance, the woman who learned to break dishes every time she was angry with her husband. She hasn't figured out yet how to move from reaction to response. In truth, when she gets angry she doesn't have to break the dishes. There are many other things she could do in response to her angry feelings—take a brisk walk, assertively communicate with her husband, take a time-out, or listen to soothing music.

Once we understand that a feeling does not necessarily led to any particular behavior, we can give ourselves permission to feel angry. Many people find this concept liberating—to discover that specific actions and feelings are not necessarily connected.

As we have discovered, our feelings constantly shift with the flow of outside events. When the baby is screaming at 4:00 a.m., your boss is in a surly mood, your best friend insults you, or your car has a flat tire, it is natural to have negative feelings associated with these things. The flexible person notices these feelings, accepts them and then chooses what to do next.

We can attend to the screaming infant, knowing that we can feel sleepy and still attend to business tomorrow morning. Instead of complaining about what a jerk the boss is, we can look for the underlying problem that sparked her anger and find a way to solve it. You can talk to your friend about the insult, maybe he didn't mean what he said the way you heard it, or you could elect to laugh it off. And the flat tire? You can accept that this is one of those things that happens that is beyond your control, and proceed to get it fixed.

Using these three steps—changing your attitude, regulating your emotions, and trying alternative behaviors—can give you powerful and effective tools to start responding instead of reacting to your life stresses. Once acquired, they can be life-changing for many people. But, like most new skills, they take practice to master. The following exercise should give you some of that practice and increase your confidence in your ability to use these newly acquired skills.

> *Once we understand that a feeling does not necessarily lead to any particular behavior, we can give ourselves permission to feel angry.*

> *When the baby is screaming at 4:00 a.m., your boss is in a surly mood, your best friend insults you, or your car has a flat tire, it is natural to have negative feelings associated with these things. The flexible person notices these feelings, accepts them and then chooses what to do next.*

Situation #1:
You feel self-conscious and unattractive.

Usual reaction: Withdraw from people, act in a negative and avoidant way toward others

Usual Outcome: Others behave negatively toward you and keep away. This reinforces your belief that you are unattractive and you feel more depressed

New responses: _____

_____

_____

Possible New Outcomes: _____

_____

_____

Situation #2:
Your partner writes a check from your joint account that bounces.

Usual reaction: Upset, angry, outraged, embarrassed, feel helpless, scared of consequences

Usual Outcome: Partner gets defensive, has numerous excuses for why it happened, blames you

New responses: _____

_____

_____

_____

Possible New Outcomes: _____

_____

_____

One of the challenges in behaving differently is... coming up with ideas about other ways we can behave in a situation. There is a strong tendency to repeat our past and do things as we have learned to do them —often starting in our childhood — without questioning or challenging what we do.

Situation #3:

You make a bad decision regarding your teenage child. Child accuses you of being unfair, a bad parent, motivated to destroy his/her life, etc.

Usual reaction: You blame, get defensive, call them ungrateful, secretly feel guilty inside

Usual Outcome: Both you and your child feel terrible, and distanced from each other.

New responses: Apologize, tell your child you made a mistake, share that parents are not perfect

Possible New Outcomes: _____

_____

_____

_____

Situation #4:

You try assertive communication with a family member, but they say, "I don't care how you feel," and they don't change or respond to your efforts.

Usual reaction: Try harder, convince yourself you are the problem.

Usual Outcome: They continue their behavior. You continue to have your feelings and issues with them

New responses: _____

_____

_____

_____

Possible New Outcomes: You no longer have the stress of their behavior. You feel much better about yourself.

> *Most would agree that one of the unique characteristics of human beings, as opposed to other animals, is the ability to have choices in how we deal with things that happen to us—even if the emotions that are triggered in us are not 100% under our control when they first occur.*

Situation #5:

You and your partner constantly argue and bicker over different parenting ideas and philosophies.

Usual reaction: Arguments, negative feelings, conflict.

Usual Outcome: Same arguments you have been having for 15 years. Neither can change how you parent

New responses: _____

_____

_____

_____

Possible New Outcomes: Harmony, stop fighting, more at peace with each other

NOTES

_____

_____

_____

_____

_____

_____

_____

_____

_____

_____

_____

_____

_____

_____

_____

_____

_____

_____

_____

_____

_____

_____

_____

_____

_____

Anger Control Tool #4
Change That Conversation with Yourself

> **Negative self-talk is often painful, harmful to our self-esteems, and sends us in a downward spiral.**

"For some reason whenever I get up set I am always putting myself down", said one woman in our group. "Even my friends tell me I am just too hard on myself," she said. "When I get upset, I will often say things like, 'I'm such a loser', or 'if I don't make it one time, everyone will think I'm a jerk,'" the woman explained. "Some times I even tell myself that I am worthless and stupid when I make mistakes." She continued, "It really makes me feel awful and angry at myself." What this woman is experiencing is a pattern of negative "self-talk." Negative self-talk is often painful, harmful to our self-esteem, and sends us in a downward spiral.

On the other hand, positive "self-talk" is a powerful tool to break the cycle of negativity that can often pollute our minds when we get angry, stressed, depressed, or feel anxious. We all have a voice in our mind that tells us messages and stories about situations in our lives. It is our self-talk that can often determine how we feel and think about a situation. The more positive our self-talk, the more positive we start to view situations.

We once had a client who told us that the way he started to feel better was to hear the words from the movie soundtrack for *Rocky*. Anyone who knows this soundtrack will often smile when they think of this tune and lyrics. Positive self-talk comes in many forms, and we will explore the use of self-talk as well as changing the way we think, behave, and feel in this chapter.

> *Learning to change that 'self-talk' empowers you to deal with anger more effectively in terms of how strongly you feel the anger, how long you hold onto your anger, and what you do as a result of your anger.*

We strongly believe that, as human beings, we are responsible for our own behavior. This is especially true with regard to control and expression of angry feelings. While angry feelings may certainly be triggered by any number of frustrating events or people in our world, it is still up to you to decide how "angry" things make you, and how you are going to deal with those angry feelings.

A crucial tool in dealing with these angry feelings is changing that conversation with yourself. Although you may not realize it, you are constantly telling yourself all kinds of things that cause you to have certain feelings or emotions. Learning to change that "self-talk" empowers you to deal with anger more effectively in terms of how strongly you feel the anger, how long you hold onto your anger, and what you do as a result of your anger.

Taking Personal Responsibility

The first step in changing that conversation with yourself is to take responsibility for your feelings, rather than blaming others or situations for how you are feeling. This is not easy, because we live in a society that teaches us to blame others or outside events for our feelings, rather than teaching us personal responsibility for our emotions.

The following is a list of common "self-talk" statements that most people have that indicates not taking responsibility for feelings—and more accurate empowering self-statements suggested for dealing with anger.

(1) **Typical self-statement**
He made me mad.

More accurate self-statements, taking personal responsibility
I made myself mad. I made myself madder than I needed to.

(2) **Typical self-statement**
It got me upset.

More accurate self-statements, taking personal responsibility
I upset myself. I upset myself more than necessary.

(3) **Typical self-statement**
My family disturbed me.

More accurate self-statements, taking personal responsibility
I disturbed myself about my family. I let them disturb me again.

(4) **Typical self-statement**
They got under my skin.

More accurate self-statements, taking personal responsibility
I let them get under my skin. I let them get under my skin more than was necessary.

(5) **Typical self-statement**
She shouldn't upset me that way

More accurate self-statements, taking personal responsibility
Better that I not upset myself. Better that I control how upset I get.

Challenge Automatic Thinking

Automatic thinking is a self-thought we automatically have in certain situations based on beliefs we have about our world. Automatic thinking occurs in the following way: it's as simple as ABC (and then we add DE to make it more powerful).

A = An event or adversity in life

Example: On the road you are delayed by an elderly woman driver in front of you going ten miles an hour below the speed limit.

B = Your beliefs and automatic thoughts about the situation

Example: What a jerk; she has no right to do that to me; I'm going to get even; she did that to me on purpose; why does she disrespect me like that; why does this always happen to me? Why can't she get out of my way?

C = Feelings, emotions

Example: Frustration, anger, outrage

D = Challenging self-talk

Example: She is not driving slowly to make me late; she probably isn't even aware of me; maybe she is old and impaired and is doing the best she can; perhaps she just came from the doctor's office with bad news and she is on the verge of tears; how would I feel toward her if I discovered the driver was my mother?

E = New effects of looking at things differently

Examples: Increased tolerance and more understanding of possible reasons for the slow driving; resolve not to take it personally; understanding that getting even to right the wrong of another driver

> *Automatic thinking is a self-thought we automatically have in certain situations, based on beliefs we have about our world.*

Take a look at some of your personal beliefs

Others have a right to be wrong.

- ☐ **I believe**
- ☐ **I don't believe**
- ☐ **Not sure**

Others should do what they want; not what I want.

- ☐ **I believe**
- ☐ **I don't believe**
- ☐ **Not sure**

I can stand it when others act badly.

- ☐ **I believe**
- ☐ **I don't believe**
- ☐ **Not sure**

People have a right to see things differently than I do.

- ☐ **I believe**
- ☐ **I don't believe**
- ☐ **Not sure**

Others do not have to treat me fairly.

- ☐ **I believe**
- ☐ **I don't believe**
- ☐ **Not sure**

If I am nice to others they have to be nice back.

- ☐ **I believe**
- ☐ **I don't believe**
- ☐ **Not sure**

Continued on the Following Page >

is not justified or rational; understanding that maintaining a hostile attitude on the road is harmful to society, innocent drivers, their families, and their loved ones.

Learning to think in these new ways is always a challenge for most people because it doesn't seem natural, and many times it doesn't even seem true. This is because our first thoughts are automatic, based on beliefs we have about the world around us.

A powerful way to learn think in this ABCDE model (first developed by a famous psychologist named Dr. Albert Ellis) is to first look at some of your assumptions or beliefs and then consider changing them if they produce anger, resentment, or unhappiness for you.

Listen to yourself as you think about things that make you angry and then see if you can talk yourself out of that anger by challenging your beliefs and then substituting new self-talk that reduces those angry feelings.

The following are some examples of new self-talk that has helped many others deal with their anger. Please check those that you think might work for you.

☐ Others have a right to their faults.

☐ It is not essential that life and other people in my world be kind to me.

☐ People are going to be the way they are and I need not get upset over this.

☐ Humans can often do the wrong thing.

☐ Others have a right to do things that I consider stupid or wrong.

☐ I am not 100% right and he or she is not 100% wrong on any matter of dispute.

☐ Others have free-will and can willfully and freely do things against my personal values.

☐ Others will treat me as they choose to, not how I choose them to.

☐ I'm not totally helpless and can go to bat for myself.

☐ As much as I would like others to be reliable, it does not mean that they must.

☐ I hope to do well, but it is not essential that I do so at every turn.

www.centuryangermanagement.com / Copyright 2005

(Continued from the Previous Page)

Take a look at some of your personal beliefs

Nice people sometimes act badly.

- ☐ **I believe**
- ☐ **I don't believe**
- ☐ **Not sure**

People have a right to betray and trespass on my values.

- ☐ **I believe**
- ☐ **I don't believe**
- ☐ **Not sure**

Others can be as different from me as they choose.

- ☐ **I believe**
- ☐ **I don't believe**
- ☐ **Not sure**

Because I'm not the General Manager of the Universe (yet), others do not necessarily have to do what I tell them to do.

- ☐ **I believe**
- ☐ **I don't believe**
- ☐ **Not sure**

I don't have to have my own way.

- ☐ **I believe**
- ☐ **I don't believe**
- ☐ **Not sure**

Others have a right to not accept me and to judge me badly.

- ☐ **I believe**
- ☐ **I don't believe**
- ☐ **Not sure**

- ☐ People will draw their own conclusions about me. It would be wise for me to accept that some will put me in good standing while others won't.

- ☐ I can deal with disappointments without turning them into disasters.

- ☐ Things don't always have to go my way.

- ☐ I can stay calm and I can handle this.

Think like an Optimist

Jane and Anthony have differing ways of viewing the world. Jane is a pessimist (the glass is half-empty), while Anthony is an optimist (the glass is half-full). These outlooks influence how they experience similar situations.

Scenario 1: Job loss

Jane is devastated, convincing herself that she is all washed up, she can never catch a break, it is useless for her to try to be successful, and she is never going to succeed at anything.

Anthony, however, has a healthier inner dialog. He tells himself he may not have been good at that particular job, his skills and company's needs did not mesh, and being fired was only a temporary setback in his career.

Scenario 2: New jobs

Offered a new job, Jane, the pessimist, believes she was able to find a new job only because her industry is now really desperate for people, and must have lowered their standards to hire her.

Anthony, however, feels he landed the new job because his talents were finally recognized and he can now be appreciated for what he can do.

Implications

As these examples illustrate, optimists tend to interpret their troubles as transient, controllable and specific to situations. Recent research by Dr. Marvin Seligman confirms this. When good things happen, optimists believe the causes are permanent, resulting from traits and abilities. Optimists further believe that good events will enhance everything they do. Pessimists, on the other hand, believe their troubles will last forever, will undermine everything they do, and believe their troubles are basically beyond their control. When good things happen to pessimists, they see them as temporary and caused by specific factors that will eventually change and lead to negative outcomes.

> *Optimism creates better resistance to depression when bad events strike, better performance at work, and better physical health.*

Benefits of Optimism

Optimism creates better resistance to depression when bad events strike, better performance at work, and better physical health. In fact, one long term study at the Mayo clinic in Rochester, MN, found that optimists lived 19% longer than pessimists.

Optimism is also a powerful antidote to anger. Many participants in our anger management classes report their anger lessening as they learn to replace negative thinking with positive thinking.

Good News for Negative Thinkers

You can learn how to replace pessimism with optimism. The starting point is to access your vulnerability to pessimistic thinking by taking the self evaluation test you can find at **www.authentichappiness.org.**

Your responses will be compared to thousands of other people in various categories, down to your zip code. If you scored lower than you'd like, you can become more optimistic. As Dr. Seligman writes in *Authentic Happiness,* his latest book: *"The trait of optimism is changeable and learnable."*

Learning to be An Optimist

There is now a well-documented method for building optimism. It's based on first recognizing *and then disputing* pessimistic thoughts.

People often do not pay attention to their thoughts and thus do not recognize how destructive they can be in leading to negative emotions.

The key is to recognize your pessimistic thoughts and then treat them *as if they were uttered by someone else*—an external person, *a rival,* whose mission in life is to make you miserable! Basically, you can become an optimist by *learning to disagree with yourself*— challenging your pessimistic thinking patterns and replacing them with more positive patterns.

> *"While everyone experiences both setbacks and victories in the normal course of life, optimists— in contrast to pessimists— have a very distinct style of explaining things to themselves."*

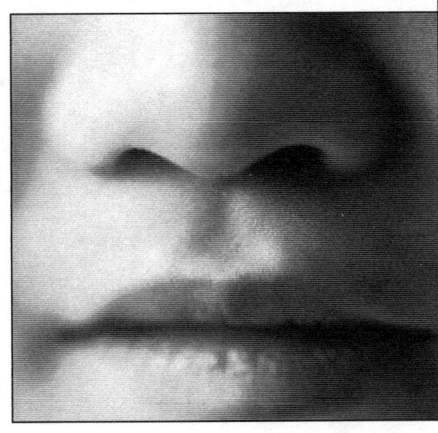

Note: this view of optimistic thinking is *not* the process of "positive thinking" in the sense of repeating silly affirmations that you really don't believe. Rather, it is the process of *correcting distorted or faulty thinking patterns* that create health, career, and relationship problems for you.

By teaching yourself to think about things *differently,* but just as realistically, you can morph yourself from a pessimist to an optimist— and tame your anger in the process.

Four Ways to Argue with Yourself

At its core, optimism is a style of interpreting events that occur in your world. It is a your personal theory or explanation of why both good things and bad things happen to you.

While everyone experiences both setbacks and victories in the normal course of life, optimists—in contrast to pessimists—have a very distinct style of explaining things to themselves.

Said another way: *It is your belief about what happens to you that determines your reaction, more than the event itself.*

The knack of disputing your beliefs is a thought-skill, the mastery of which will morph you into the optimistic style of thinking. There are four ways to do this:

1. Look at the evidence

According to Seligman, the most convincing way of disputing a negative belief is to show that it is factually incorrect.

Most of the time you will have "reality" on your side. Your role is that of a detective as you ask, "what is the evidence for my belief?" For example, is it *really* true that you never succeed in anything? (Very doubtful. Everybody succeeds some of the time.) That you are the *worse parent* you know? (Can you remember any success you have had as a parent?) That you are an incurable *glutton*? (Can you sometimes resist food?) That you are incredibly *selfish*? (How many times have you been unselfish?)

Using this skill of looking at the evidence, you can defeat pessimism with more accurate perception and recall what is *really* true.

To illustrate this, try the following exercise.

List a negative belief or self-talk that you have that causes anger, sadness, or resentment in you.

_____

_____

_____

_____

_____

_____

> **Evidence that shows your negative belief may not be true or not always true.**

Now, what evidence do you have that this belief is true?

_____

_____

_____

_____

_____

_____

Pretending that you are a "detective," can you find evidence to the contrary, evidence that shows your negative belief may not be true or not always true? Be honest and list the evidence, even if you are not yet convinced that it disproves your negative belief.

_____

_____

_____

_____

_____

_____

44

> *If the facts are NOT on your side and you cannot honestly see other causes of a negative event, you will need to look at the implications of your beliefs to become an optimistic thinker.*

2. Consider alternative causes

Most events in the world have more than one cause. Pessimists latch onto the most insidious; optimists tend more to give themselves a break.

For example, a marital breakup usually has many causes that probably contributed to its downfall. You can blame yourself. You can blame your partner. A more optimistic interpretation is that neither partner failed as an individual; it was the *relationship* that failed.

Continuing with our exercise, try to come up with other events or circumstances that may have contributed to the negative outcome

_____

_____ could have contributed to the event.

_____

_____ could have contributed to the event.

_____

_____ could have contributed to the event.

3. Put events into perspective

If the facts are NOT on your side and you cannot honestly see other causes of a negative event, you will need to look at the *implications* of your beliefs to become an *optimistic* thinker.

Is the event *really* as catastrophic as you may be making it in your mind? Here's a hint: a few things are. Usually, the implications or long-term effects of your misfortune aren't as awful or devastating as you may be seeing them.

To think more optimistically, you could view the impact of the negative event in a different way that would decrease your anger. Describe how you might put the event in proper perspective.

_____

_____

_____

> *Even though a belief may, in fact, be true, it may not be useful. Some beliefs cause more grief than they are worth.*

_____

_____

_____

_____

_____

_____

_____

4. Is your belief useful?

Even though a belief may, in fact, be true, it may not be useful. Some beliefs cause more grief than they are worth. You may tell yourself you are a failure, for instance. This belief will likely cause to you stop trying. Instead, substitute a more useful belief like "Just because I failed once doesn't make me a failure." Then, behave accordingly with your new belief.

To illustrate this principal, try thinking of more useful beliefs you could acquire about negative events or even failures in your life.

More useful belief #1

_____

_____

_____

_____

_____

_____

_____

_____

_____

_____

More useful belief #2

_____

_____

_____

_____

_____

_____

_____

_____

_____

_____

> *Usually, the implications or long-term effects of your misfortune aren't as awful or devastating as you may be seeing them.*

NOTES

_____

_____

_____

_____

_____

_____

_____

_____

_____

_____

_____

_____

_____

_____

_____

_____

_____

_____

_____

_____

_____

Anger Control Tool #5
Assertive Communication

> *Learning to express your primary feelings and needs clearly, calmly, and with good eye contact is what assertive communication is all about.*

Our client, Aaron, told us that in his family they typically yell at one another to get a point across. Aaron recently got in a relationship with a woman who told him that his anger "scares" her when he gets upset. Aaron's reply was that he was not upset, this was "just the way I am used to expressing myself when I get upset, this is normal for me". The reality is that what might be "normal" for you and your family of origin may not be the "norm" when it comes to communicating effectively with others. Aaron's style of communication is aggressive, but he didn't realize the impact it had on his girlfriend. Aaron had to learn about his style of communication as well as other styles of communication to understand the kind of changes he needed to make. By learning to become more assertive, Aaron felt better, his needs got met more of the time, and his girlfriend no longer feared him when he did get upset.

The way we communicate or the style we use to communicate is often learned from much earlier experiences in our lives when our language skills were newly formed. Think about your family's style of communication for a moment. Is your style similar to any of your family members'? Most of us tend to communicate in a way that was adaptive in the environment we grew up, but problematic in our lives today. For many of us, our style of communication can leave us with unmet needs, unexpressed emotion, and damaging effects on those around us. It is important to understand that there are many different communication styles, yet only one that tends to yield the results we are seeking. Learning to express your primary feelings and needs clearly, calmly, and with good eye contact is what assertive communication is

> *Some patterns are negative and harmful while others are positive and productive.*

all about.

Good communication skills are an essential ingredient in anger management because poor communication causes untold emotional hurt, misunderstandings, and conflict. Words are powerful, but the message we convey to others is even more powerful and often determines how people respond to us, and how we feel toward them.

Because communication is a two-way process, people with good communication skills are good at "receiving" messages from others as well as delivering them.

If you look at people in your life and also look at your own behavior, you may discover certain patterns of communication. Some patterns are negative and harmful while others are positive and productive.

Frequently persons who have anger problems use harmful ways of communicating to others. Harmful in the sense that it disrupts relationships and usually does not accomplish your goals.

Assertive communication, on the other hand, is a much more effective way to get what you want and what you need without the negative consequences. In short, developing assertive communication skills will work for you by making you a more effective and less stressed person.

Let's start by looking at the harmful patterns first and then at the assertive remedies that we have found to really work for many of the participants in our anger management classes and seminars.

Harmful Communication Styles

Harmful communication patterns are usually those that occur in people's lives before they start anger management classes. Harmful communication patterns also are predictors of divorce and partner conflict.

Let's review some of these patterns:

Harmful Pattern #1 – Avoidance

In marital research this is also called "stonewalling." While it may occur in both genders, it is more characteristic of men than women. Basically, it means being emotionally unavailable—cutting yourself off emotionally from the person you have an issue with. It can also mean not dealing with an issue by changing the topic, ignoring the other when they speak to you, or doing something else (like watching television) when your partner tries to discuss important things with you.

www.centuryangermanagement.com / Copyright 2005

Example: *Stacy and Bill were married for twenty years and had an eleven year old daughter. About four times a year, Stacy would go into a rage over a minor event in the household, and Bill could not cope with his wife's behavior when this occurred. For weeks afterward he would not talk to her. He basically ignored her despite her apologies and numerous attempts to emotionally connect with him.*

Why do you think this is a harmful communication pattern?

_____

_____

_____

_____

_____

> ## *Being overly critical toward others is a harmful communication pattern because it puts other people on the defensive and causes them to have negative feelings toward you.*

Harmful Pattern #2 – Criticism

Being overly critical toward others (or toward ourselves) is a harmful communication pattern because it puts other people on the defensive and causes them to have negative feelings toward you. It is another communication pattern that predicts divorce—especially if it occurs with married women.

Does this mean we can never complain about things or let people know we are dissatisfied with them or their behavior? Of course not. But to communicate effectively, we need to complain in a certain way. A complaint is a specific statement of anger, distress, displeasure or other negativity. Criticism involves attacking someone's personality or character, rather than a specific behavior. In relationships, a criticism takes a complaint and adds blame. It *feels* like you as a person are being attacked or judged by the other person.

The fact is, most people cannot deal with too much criticism over a long period of time. Unfortunately, often highly critical people don't see themselves that way. Rather they truly think they are "helping" their partner in some way by constantly pointing out defects in his/her character and inadequacies.

Yet, constant, unfair, or high-volume criticism starts to just feel bad after awhile and erodes self-esteem as well as positive feelings toward someone you previously may have loved or at least liked a lot.

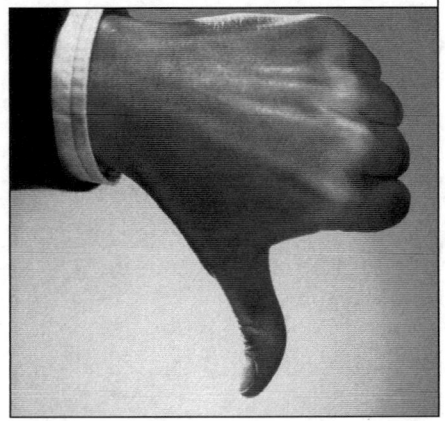

Do you think men or women can better handle criticism from their partners?

_____

_____

_____

_____

_____

Why do you think this is so?

_____

_____

_____

_____

_____

The passive-aggressive pattern is a harmful, covert way of communicating angry feelings, but indirectly, and sometimes without you knowing that you are doing it!

Harmful Pattern #3 – Passive-Aggression

The passive-aggressive pattern is a harmful, covert way of communicating angry feelings, but indirectly, and sometimes without you knowing that you are doing it! It is a way of getting back at people without telling them why, instead of confronting them head-on.

Often, the passive-aggressive communicator is trying to manipulate you or some situation in an underhanded way.

For instance, we might make a joke at someone else' expense. Or, we might make sarcastic remarks that communicate hostility or other negative feelings that we have.

The passive-aggressive communicator may also sabotage us or our efforts, but in a way that is difficult to prove that that is what they are doing. When confronted, they will often deny that they are angry with you or that they are doing anything to harm you.

www.centuryangermanagement.com / Copyright 2005

Often, the passive-aggressive communicator is trying to manipulate you or some situation in an under-handed way.

Examples of harmful, passive-aggressive behaviors:

- When talking with someone you are angry with, leaving out important information that gives the wrong impression.

- Talking behind the back of a co-worker in a harmful way—gossiping.

- Husband getting home late without calling, resulting in his wife missing an important meeting; then he pleads he was late because he was "helping a friend."

- Wife "forgetting" (for the first time) to pick up the husband's suit at the dry cleaners that he desperately needs for the next business day—following an evening when they argued over their love life.

- Exaggerating the faults of your spouse (behind his or her back) to your parents.

- Playing dumb to frustrate someone or gain advantage.

- Clamming up and not talking to someone because you are angry.

- Arguing for the sake of arguing to escape dealing with the real issue.

Another form of passive-aggressive anger is "perpetual victimhood." Afraid to confront the source of anger, the person feels victimized and feels persecuted. They feel there is nothing they can do to change the situation and they accept no responsibility.

What are some other examples of passive-aggressive communicating?

_____

_____

_____

_____

_____

_____

_____

_____

_____

Harmful Pattern #4 – Aggression

A certain amount of aggression in some situations is acceptable, but some people consistently charge around like a bull in a china shop to get what they want and this is extremely harmful to good communication. Overly aggressive people like to have things their own way and often express feelings in a way that punishes or intimidates (scares) others.

Aggressive people tend to communicate by getting "in your face." They get too close to you or they stand while you are seated so they can dominate you. Often, they relate to you in a loud voice. They may gesture wildly. You may feel scolded or intimidated. They may give you orders with no thought for your feelings.

Have you ever been aggressive in your behavior?

_____

_____

_____

Have you ever tried to get your own way no matter what you had to do to get it?

_____

_____

_____

Have you ever threatened someone in a way that caused bad feelings?

_____

_____

_____

Harmful Pattern #5 – Defensiveness

Defensiveness is a communication style that people use to emotionally protect themselves rather than to openly listen to others or to honestly express their own feelings. Defensive people are not able to accept influence from others, especially intimate partners, and therefore it is another predictor of divorce. Defensive people have a force-field or shell around them that prevents them from being able to take personal responsibility for conflicts or problems with others. Defensive people are not open to feedback from others and are not open to changing or

> *Overly aggressive people like to have things their own way and often express feelings in a way that punishes or intimidates (scares) others.*

The Look of Contempt

Research shows that when people are feeling contempt, it is expressed in their face by the left hand corner of their mouth pulled to create a "dimple."

> *Defensive people have a force-field or shell around them which prevents them from being able to take personal responsibility for conflict or problems with others.*

improving themselves. They see no need to change themselves. They take criticism very personally and are easily offended by even mild criticism or suggestions by others. They are emotionally fragile and don't want to hear things that don't "fit" their view of how things are.

Do you know of anyone who is defensive? How do they act?

_____

_____

_____

_____

What challenges have you found in relating to such a person?

_____

_____

_____

_____

_____

_____

Harmful Pattern #6 – Contempt

Contempt is a communication style of regarding someone or something as inferior or less-than. In effect, we look down on them. Even worse, sometimes it means treating others with scorn as if we regard them as worthless.

When we are treated with contempt by others we feel despised, dishonored or disgraced.

It is a very destructive way to relate to others; not surprisingly, it is a major predictor of divorce, according to recent research.

Some common "contemptuous" behaviors include:

• Name-calling, swearing, or disrespecting partner

• Denying the importance of another's feelings

• Moralizing or preaching

- Saying hurtful, mean-spirited things

- Insulting partner or family in a way that causes emotional injury

- Humiliating or ridiculing partner in front of children or others

- Putting pressure on others to do things against one's core values

The Assertive Communicator

What is assertive communication?

It is a way to communicate so that you convey your rights in a good way. Assertive communication helps people clearly explain their wants, needs, and feelings to other people. It is a way of getting things that you want without violating or offending others' rights or having to walk away without getting what you want.

Assertive people tell others what they want and need clearly; they have a knack of saying the correct thing at the correct time.

Assertive communication skills are the antidote to harmful and destructive communication patterns.

There are six steps to assertive communication. Each of these steps is a remedy to the harmful communication patterns that we just discussed.

Assertive Remedy #1 – Send Clear Messages

The assertive communicators send clear messages, making sure that the message received is the message you send. Research shows that about 80% of the "message" communicated is done without words by your "non-verbal" behavior. If your words say one thing, but your body language says something else, the listener may be quite confused.

It's not always what you say that people respond to, but how you say it.

Pay close attention to:
- Facial expressions
- Eye Contact
- Posture (how you stand)
- Hand and arm movement
- Tone of Voice

What are some ways that "tone of voice" can influence your commu-

> *Assertive people tell others what they want and need clearly; they have a knack of saying the correct thing at the correct time.*

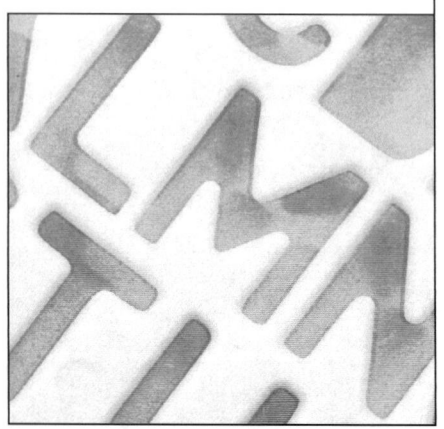

Take an inventory of listening skills that you have or need to develop

Not judging others as they speak.

☐ **I have**
☐ **I need to develop**

Focusing on what speaker is attempting to communicate.

☐ **I have**
☐ **I need to develop**

Giving speaker your full attention.

☐ **I have**
☐ **I need to develop**

Pausing and think before answering.

☐ **I have**
☐ **I need to develop**

Restate what the other person is saying in order to clarify.

☐ **I have**
☐ **I need to develop**

Have good eye contact.

☐ **I have**
☐ **I need to develop**

Don't let your mind wander.

☐ **I have**
☐ **I need to develop**

Focus on the meaning of what the speaker is saying as well as content of words.

☐ **I have**
☐ **I need to develop**

Be sensitive to the unspoken feelings in the speaker's message.

☐ **I have**
☐ **I need to develop**

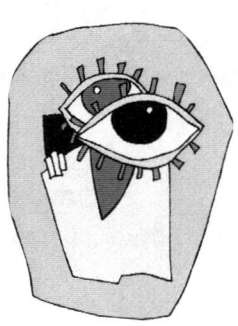

nication with someone?

_____

_____

_____

_____

_____

What type of eye contact should we have for best communication? Why is eye contact important?

_____

_____

_____

_____

_____

Assertive remedy #2 – Learn How to Listen

Assertive people have developed their listening skills. As you may have noticed, most people do not have very good listening skills. In fact, rather than really listening to you, many people unfortunately listen with their answer running—meaning that they are thinking of a response rather than listening deeply to what you are saying.

Hearing is done with our ears while listening is done with our heart. Listening is an active process. The listener must take an active role in the communication process.

Assertive Remedy #3 – Express Complaints By Using the "Magical Formula"

Words have tremendous power to determine how other people experience us and how they respond to us. People with good assertive communication skills focus on the problem behavior (and not the character of the person), stick to the point, don't use labels, and make "I" statements rather than "you" statements.

The process to do this can be put into this formula:

> **Words have tremendous power to determine how other people experience us, and how they respond to us.**

I feel …*describe the feeling you are having.*

When you…*describe the behavior that bothers you*

Because…*describe how the behavior affects you*

I need…*how you are requesting the person to change*

Example #1: *Your husband was supposed to be home at 7:00 p.m., but does not show up until 8:30—with no phone call. Try communicating your justifiable complaint in the following way:*

" I **feel** (angry) **when you** (don't phone when you are going to be late) **because** (I worry about you). I **need** you (to be more considerate of my feelings)."

Example #2: *You walk by a work station and a co-worker whom you consider a friend is joking to someone about your recent divorce.*

"I **felt** (disrespected and hurt) **when you** (joked about my divorce to my co-workers) **because** (it is a sensitive issue to me and I've always considered you a friend). I **need** (for you to not make jokes about that anymore and to keep what I tell you confidential).

Example #3: *You are visiting your family over the holidays. Your mother remarks critically once again how you need to lose weight.*

Mom, I know you love me and want what is best for me, but I **feel** so bad about myself and resentment toward you when you bring up my weight **because** I am doing the best I can. Please don't bring it up again because **I need** for us to be friends and for you to recognize how hard I am trying.

Does this formula work every time? Of course not. And there are times when it is clearly inappropriate to use. Also, you must be careful not to use it too much, or it may appear manipulative to the other person.

But, it does work a high percentage of the time and it should be always be tried first before communicating the same complaint in an angry way. The "formula," when used correctly, can convey a dissatisfaction or problem in a way that makes it a complaint and *not a criticism* and that often allows the other person to "hear" you without getting defensive or feeling attacked.

In intimate relationships, the "formula" serves as a "softened startup" —a way to approach each other over an issue without feeling attacked and causing so much conflict.

It is important to remember that not all people respond well to assertive

communicators. People who tend to be more passive or passive-aggressive in their own communication styles may feel threatened by someone who is asserting their position.

Example: *When your coworker decides to smoke a cigarette in the break room while you are there taking your break, you assert your position by stating:*

"When you smoke in here, I feel dizzy because I am allergic to cigarette smoke. I know that this is also your break period and so I would just ask that you smoke in the designated area."

You asserted your message and the other person is defensive—maybe outraged. What do you do next? The following are steps to take when dealing with this kind of situation.

(1) Take the time to prepare your assertion calmly and sensitively.

(2) Offer the message to the other person. Do not hurl it.

(3) Use the silence as the initial response to the defensive reaction. Listen to the response and take time to consider yours.

(4) Actively listen to the other person. This reassures and invites them to collaborate.

(5) Recycle your assertion. It is still without blame and shows your desire to continue working on a solution.

(6) Always keep focused on a mutual solution.

Assertive Remedy #4 – Acknowledge Your Part in Conflicts

Anger is often an escalating process, involving two people who create negative feelings in each other, sometimes instantly, and sometimes over a long period of time.

When this happens, it is natural to blame the other person entirely for the problem, especially when we are angry and in a defensive mode. But, once we return to normal, the assertive communicator is able to accept some of the responsibility for the conflict.

Taking some responsibility is an indication of emotional maturity and is an antidote or a remedy to defensiveness. You never win an emotional argument with facts, figures, or excessive logic.

> *People who tend to be more passive or passive-aggressive in their own communication styles may feel threatened by someone who is asserting their position.*

Handling Conflicts

Often, conflicts become unmanageable because of the thoughts and emotions that get involved. Automatic thoughts, that is, those thoughts that have no real evidence to support them, are often the cause of unresolved conflicts. These thoughts can lead to incorrect assumptions about the situation or the persons involved in the conflict.

Emotions can also get in the way of conflict resolution. Often when misunderstood, people can be left feeling angry, hurt, afraid, confused, envious, etc. These emotions can lead to further automatic thoughts, thus perpetuating the conflict.

Conflict Resolution Approaches

A conflict resolution approach is the method or manner in which a person attempts to eliminate or minimize a conflict between the persons involved. Negotiation and mediation are conflict resolution approaches. They are not, however, the only way people resolve conflicts.

There are five main approaches to resolving conflict. Some are more passive than others. Some are aggressive. The last approach deals with collaborating with the other person in the conflict. This is the approach we will be learning in this section of the Anger Management Program.

- **Avoiding** occurs when one or both people recognize that a conflict exists. They respond by withdrawing from the conflict. This is a relatively passive approach.

- **Accommodating** occurs when one person resolves the conflict by giving in to the other person at the expense of his or her own needs. When one side has overwhelming power and the will to use it, the person with less power will tend to accommodate. This approach is also passive.

- **Compromising** occurs when both people gain and lose in order to resolve the conflict. It is an approach in which gains and losses are shared. Each person is partially satisfied and partially dissatisfied. In a continuing relationship, both people need to preserve face and continue their relationship. Therefore, sharing partial victory and partial defeat can meet mutual needs. This is also a passive approach, although it leans more towards assertiveness since each are asserting their rights in the conflict. However, they must give up something in order for the conflict to be resolved. This is where it becomes passive.

> *Often, conflicts become unmanageable because of the thoughts and emotions that get involved.*

www.centuryangermanagement.com / Copyright 2005

> *Many times you need to decide if you want to be right or you want to be happy.*

- **Forcing** occurs when one or both people attempt to satisfy their own needs regardless of the impact to the other person. It is an aggressive "no holds barred" approach.

Forcing can produce victories at excessive cost to the winner. Winning by forcing damages ongoing relationships, thus destroying the possibility of future cooperation. The loser tends to seek revenge in passive-aggressive ways to balance the scales. War is a prime example of using the forcing approach to resolve conflict.

- **Collaborating** is an attempt made by both people to fully satisfy the needs of each. With collaboration, each individual is a winner. This approach assumes that each person involved in the conflict has legitimate goals and that creative thinking can transform the conflict into an opportunity for both to achieve their goals.

Collaborating, or problem solving as it is sometimes called, requires both people to look beyond the immediate problem. It takes some creativity, and usually creativity consumes time and energy. Nevertheless, a collaborating approach to conflict resolution can produce two winners and is the most assertive approach to conflict resolution.

Useful Things to Say to Resolve Conflict

Here are some things to say to the person you are in conflict with that will show you are taking some of the responsibility for the problem and that you want to work things out in a collaborative way:

- My reactions were too extreme. I'm sorry.
- Even though I still feel I was right about the issue, my reaction wasn't right and I apologize for that.
- I really blew that one.
- Let me try again.
- I can see my part in all this.
- I see your point. I know this isn't your fault.
- We are both saying that…
- This is not your problem. It is OUR problem.
- I never thought of things that way.
- I might be wrong here.
- I think your point of view makes sense.
- Let me start again in a softer way.

An exercise: *What conflict resolution patterns did you learn in your family of origin?*

(1) How did your parents resolve conflict?

_____

_____

_____

_____

_____

(2) How did you and your siblings resolve conflict?

_____

_____

_____

_____

_____

_____

(3) Things I wanted as a child, but didn't get:

_____

_____

_____

_____

_____

(4) The way I felt when I didn't get it:

_____

_____

_____

_____

_____

> *A collaborating approach to conflict resolution can produce two winners and is the most assertive approach to conflict resolution.*

(5) The way I behaved when I didn't get what I wanted:

_____

_____

_____

_____

_____

_____

_____

> *Praise is a positive remedy for both critical and contemptuous ways of communicating.*

Assertive Remedy #5 – Give and Take Praise

Praise is an important part of assertive communication, both in terms of being able to give praise and take praise. Praise is a positive remedy for both critical and contemptuous ways of communicating.

Praise involves seeing the positives, what is right, and what you can honor and appreciate about the other person. This is opposed to angry people who tend to see only what is wrong or negative about each other, and then comment about the negatives.

In relationships, being able to see things in your mate that even your friends don't see is a very positive predictor of marital success, according to recent research at the State University of New York. Remarkably, what the research shows is that satisfied couples see virtues in their partners that are not seen by their closest friends. The happiest couples look on the bright side of the relationship and focus on strengths rather than weaknesses.

On the other hand, dissatisfied couples have a "tainted" image of each other; they see fewer virtues in their mates than their friends do.

Assertive Remedy #6 – Express Feelings Openly

Expressing feelings openly is a remedy for the harmful and destructive passive-aggressive communication style.

Many angry people "store" feelings or grievances they have toward others, but unfortunately, the negative feelings often do not go away, even if they are not expressed on the surface.

It is like putting the feelings in a bottle. You try to put the lid on tightly, but some of those suppressed feelings find a way to leak out.

Summary and Checklist of Communication Patterns

Check patterns that apply and discuss remedy

Harmful Pattern:
Avoidance/Stonewalling

- ☐ **Have**
- ☐ **Don't Have**
- ☐ **Unsure**

Assertive Remedy:
Learn How to Listen

Harmful Pattern:
Criticism

- ☐ **Have**
- ☐ **Don't Have**
- ☐ **Unsure**

Assertive Remedy:
Assertive Complaint/
Magical Formula

Harmful Pattern:
Passive-Aggression

- ☐ **Have**
- ☐ **Don't Have**
- ☐ **Unsure**

Assertive Remedy:
Express Feelings Openly

Harmful Pattern:
Aggression

- ☐ **Have**
- ☐ **Don't Have**
- ☐ **Unsure**

Assertive Remedy:
Clarify Message

Harmful Pattern:
Defensiveness

- ☐ **Have**
- ☐ **Don't Have**
- ☐ **Unsure**

Assertive Remedy:
Accept Responsibility

Harmful Pattern:
Contempt

- ☐ **Have**
- ☐ **Don't Have**
- ☐ **Unsure**

Assertive Remedy:
Give and Take Praise

It is much better to deal with anger or resentment directly, before things get out of hand. If people don't know you are upset with them, how can they change?

Why are some people so hesitant to be open and emotionally honest with others, especially people close to them? Some of the reasons psychologists commonly hear are:

- I don't want to hurt their feelings

- I'm afraid of what their reaction might be

- They might start being too honest toward me

- They might "emotionally" punish me in some way by withholding something I need.

Despite these issues, it is important that you work at expressing feelings openly because assertion is impossible until you learn to express your feelings to others. Learn to do this by practicing daily. Begin with small things. Express your feelings about something that happened. Once you become comfortable in expressing your feelings, you can take bigger risks.

www.centuryangermanagement.com / Copyright 2005

NOTES

NOTES

_____

_____

_____

_____

_____

_____

_____

_____

_____

_____

_____

_____

_____

_____

_____

_____

_____

_____

_____

_____

_____

_____

_____

Anger Control Tool #6
Adjust Those Expectations

Anger and stress can often be caused when our expectations are too far apart from what is realistic to achieve.

Expectations and Anger

We once got a referral from a company that had an employee with "anger problems" at work. Her name was Sara and she was asked by her employer to attend our program to learn more skills to cope with her problem. Sara explained to us that, "I have high standards of the people that work for me," then went on, "I expect my staff to stay late, bring their work home, work over time, or whatever it takes to get the job done." Sara explained how frustrated she felt at work, as she was always let down by someone who didn't put the effort in that she felt was needed.

One approach that Sara learned through our program was the ability to adjust expectations to an appropriate level. For many of us, we expect much more that is "reasonable" in certain situations. By learning how to adjust our expectations to an appropriate level, we are often left feeling more satisfied and less frustrated in situations at work, school, with family members, and most importantly, with ourselves.

Have you ever been told your "expectations are too high?" Anger and stress can often be caused when our expectations are too far apart from what is realistic to achieve. For example, let's say you promise your mother you'll bring over your famous homemade apple pie for dinner on Friday night. You also know that Friday night you have a project due at work. Is it realistic that you will be able to get home in time to bake the pie from scratch and get to your mothers house in time? The answer…probably not. When we create expectations that

> *Anger results by mentally comparing the behavior of others to what you expected them to do or to be.*

are not realistic we often tend to feel more stressed out, angry, and let ourselves and those around us down.

Anger results by mentally comparing the behavior of others to what you expected them to do or to be. Sometimes that is a reasonable thing to do, but often it is not because we have too high or wrong expectations of ourselves and those around us.

Another way of saying this is that anger is often triggered by the difference between what we expect and what we get.

It is important to figure out exactly what "reasonable" means in terms of expectations. If expectations are too low, you will feel cheated in life, or worse, you will feel that you are "settling." On the other hand, if expectations are too high, then the reality of the experience will suffer from the comparison—and you may experience disappointment and other negative emotions such as anger.

The real cause of anger isn't all those things that happen to us, rather the root problem is in how we **assess** or **evaluate** what happens to us and how other people behave.

Does this mean that we shouldn't have expectations of others? Of course not! That would be impossible and also not very wise, since other people often will rise to the occasion if you have high expectations of them; this is true, for instance, with our children. And of course, having high expectations of yourself can often motivate you to high achievement, personal growth, and accomplishment.

But, in terms of managing your anger, you should find a way to be realistic about both the *level* of expectations you have, and the *type* of expectations you have. It is possible to have the right level of expectation of someone—but the wrong type of expectation to begin with. For instance, you could have a realistically high expectation that your child will be a professional, but as an architect instead of as a doctor.

Anger results by mentally comparing the behavior of others to what you expect them to do, to have, or to be.

If people do not meet your expectations, rather than becoming frustrated, irritated, or angry toward them, why not put them into a different "category" of your mind?

Learn to adjust both the level and the type of those expectations and you have a powerful tool for anger management. We have discovered that this is a five-step process:

68

Five Steps To Adjust Your Expectations

Step 1– Decide what is "reasonable" and what is not

This may be tricky because different people have different ideas of this. One way to do it is to think about it when you are calm and cool. Many things that seemed "reasonable" when you were worked up seem ridiculous and petty in the cold light of day. So, make yourself take a time out, and think things through before responding. It is much easier to decide what is "reasonable" or not with a clear head.

Another way to do it is to compare someone's behavior with other people in that situation or age group. For instance, we have different expectations for teens and adults, for single people and married people, for normal circumstances and difficult ones (such as grieving, or going through a divorce), for managers and minimum-wage workers, etc.

If you still are not sure if your expectation is reasonable, try asking peers or friends for honest feedback. Good friends will tell you the truth and help you adjust those expectations in line with common standards in your social group or community.

Step 2 – Take the word "should" out of your vocabulary

Fact is, we can't control other people, try as we might. People behave the way they behave for their own reasons. Avoid the trap of getting upset because others don't behave as they "should." This sets up an expectation on your part that may not be reasonable—and it may also be wrong. Instead of "shoulding" on yourself, try changing your vocabulary to words like *"I would prefer if..." "It would be nice if...,"* instead of *"They should...."*

Here are some questions to ask yourself that will help you in changing how you think about things that trigger your anger:

- Why "should" the other person do what I think they should?
- Why "should" things go the way I demand them to go?
- Am I being too demanding of others?
- Am I imposing my own viewpoint on them?
- Am I judging them because they don't do as they "should" in my mind?

> *Good friends will tell you the truth and help you adjust those expectations in line with common standards in your social group or community.*

> *People often behave badly toward us because they are limited or have a problem, not because they are purposefully trying to make us miserable.*

Step 3 – Remember that sometimes people or situations have more limitations than you give them credit for.

People often behave badly toward us because they are limited or have a problem, but not because they are purposefully trying to make us miserable. Of course, we want them to live up to our expectations, but in truth they are fallible people who may not be able to. Perhaps they have a different agenda in life besides meeting your expectations.

For example, the middle-aged woman who cuts us off on the freeway may be doing it because she just learned that her husband is divorcing her—she probably doesn't even know that you exist! Our parents may not give us the love we deserve, not because there is something wrong with us, but because they have a limited capacity to love their children in the right way. Your envious sibling may not have the capacity to "share" the limelight with other people—including you.

Other personal limitations may include psychological disorders or emotional difficulties which limit a person's ability to function adequately in certain life areas. Examples might include depression (which is why the other may not have energy), ADHD (which may prevent a person from being able to focus or stick to tasks, or achieve in school), or anxiety disorders (which may lead to social isolation).

Limitations in Relationships

Relationships also have their limitations. New marital research by the Gottman Institute in Seattle, Washington gives the startling statistic that more than two-thirds (69%) of continuing disagreements between partners are unresolvable or "perpetual problems." This means that if it was an issue on the day you met, it may still be an issue thirty years later due to differences in personality, lifestyles, and personal viewpoints.

Couples unfortunately become "gridlocked" on these issues; trying to solve the unsolvable only creates frustration, anger, and marital discontent.

Examples of perpetual issues may include differences in parenting styles, differences in religious viewpoints, differences in character traits, in personality, in sexual preferences, and in money management.

Perpetual issues that lead to gridlock are experienced by couples both in great marriages and not so great ones! The key to dealing with them is to recognize they are unsolvable, partly because many of these issues are not only about what is on the surface, but about the deeper

How Tom and Mary Handled Their Perpetual Problem

Married 13 years, Tom and Mary always fought about money management. She was a spender (mostly on things for others), while he was a saver. He tried to persuade her to save, she called him a tightwad and said he should be more giving and less self-centered about money.

They were still fighting about this on their thirteenth wedding anniversary. Seeing that this issue would never go away, they finally decided to have a talk about it. Turns out, he had a life dream of owning a home and was judging how successful his life turned out by home ownership. He paniced as he saw the home ownership opportunity slipping away.

By contrast, she was raised as a preacher's daughter and believed that it was somehow evil to save money for personal use rather than giving it away to others. She had severe guilt pangs if she had money in the savings account when it could be put to good use.

While neither changed their attitudes, after their dialogue, they had increased understanding and empathy for the other. This lead to less anger and exploration of ways they could both live out their life dreams.

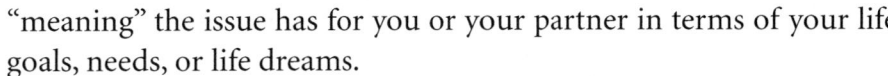

"meaning" the issue has for you or your partner in terms of your life goals, needs, or life dreams.

Rather than trying to "solve" the problem (which usually means that you expect the other person to change how they are, or your partner expects you to change how you are), accept that it will probably always be there because it is part of who you are, or part of who your partner is. Start by having a dialogue, a conversation, about it with your partner to learn how the issue is somehow tied to either their life dream or your life dream. Then, find ways to be with each other despite the issue and watch how your anger level immediately goes down.

Step 4 – Remind yourself—and this is a tough one—that the way you see things may not be how other people see the same things or events.

Rather than convincing yourself they are "wrong," tell yourself that they simply see things differently than you do. No need to get angry over this; they may be as convinced of their "truth" as you are of yours.

Did you know that all the wars in the world have resulted from a clash of two "rights?" They are never started by a "right" and a "wrong" because warring countries always see themselves as being right.

If others don't agree with you, they may honestly remember things differently than you do. For a test of this principal, have a discussion with your parents (or your children) about a past event that you remember vividly. You may be surprised and astounded at how differently you both remember the very same event.

If fact, recent memory research shows clearly that we can be dead wrong about an event we are absolutely convinced occurred exactly the way we remember it! This occurs partly because our mind modifies our memories to "fit" our beliefs or world view. After we "recall" these distorted memories a few times, they become "fact" in our mind, even though what really happened may be quite different.

So, to control your anger, adjust your expectations of others and give them a break. They may honestly be remembering things quite differently from you or they may have seen things from a different perspective than you to begin with.

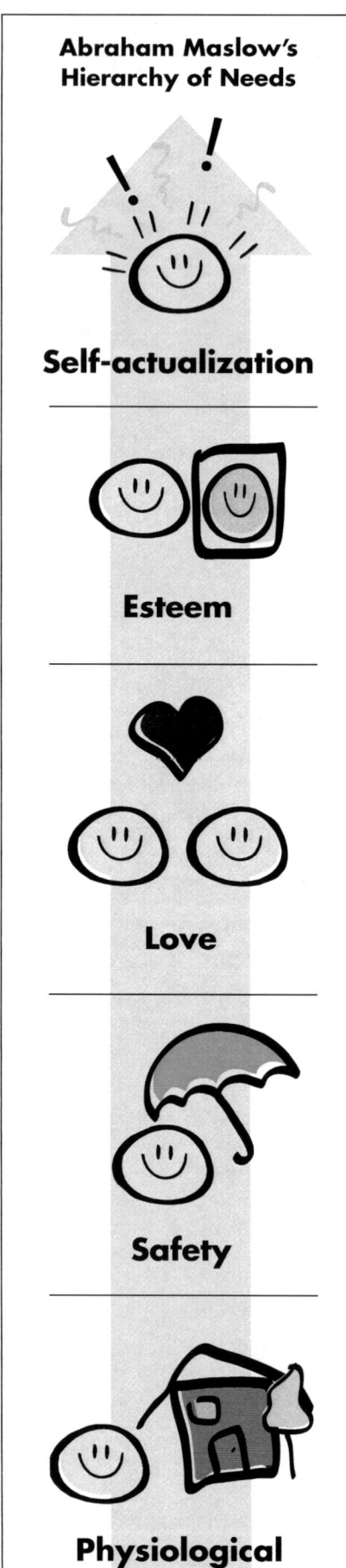

Abraham Maslow's Hierarchy of Needs

Self-actualization

Esteem

Love

Safety

Physiological

Step 5 - Find other ways to get your needs met

The underlying reason we often get angry at others or situations when our expectations are not met is because are needs are not being met as a result of the situation or the behavior of the other.

Rather than getting angry, we need to consider two other ways to deal with the situation—ways that are far more effective. First, learn to communicate your needs to the other that are not being satisfied by them not meeting your expectations. Second, find other ways to satisfy those needs.

Communicating Needs

Sometimes we don't effectively communicate our needs to people, so they don't have a clue what is underlying our anger. It is much more effective to recognize and express that underlying need rather than just getting angry. If you learn to do this, you will find that people will know better how to respond to you. We all have needs, contrary to some popular thinking; it is not selfish to recognize and try to get our needs fulfilled.

Before practicing how to do this, it may be helpful to first look at what our needs are, according to a famous psychologist named Abraham Maslow who devised a hierarchy of needs.

According to Maslow, lower needs must be met before we are capable of satisfying the next level of need. For instance, people will only be motivated to seek ways to enhance self-esteem after they are well fed, feel safe, and feel loved.

Physiological Needs

These needs are the very basic needs such as air, food, sleep, and sex. Fulfillment of these needs motivate us to alleviate them as soon as possible to get back to normal. Once satisfied, we can think about how to satisfy other, higher-order needs.

Safety Needs

Safety needs are mostly psychological in nature and have to do with establishing stability and consistency in our world. This need motivates us to try and achieve predictability in our lives—in our physical environment, in our families, and in our intimate relationships. Some people have a very high need for security in almost every aspect of their lives, while other people have a much lower need for safety; for them, excitement, adventure, or risk is much more important.

Love Needs

Most humans have a desire to belong to groups, to feel loved by others, and to be accepted by others. Once we feel secure and safe, according to Maslow, we are motivated to satisfy our love and belongingness needs.

Esteem Needs

This category includes both self-esteem (how we value ourselves) and being esteemed or valued by others. Persons with good mental health need to feel good about themselves and their lives. Much of our behavior is directed toward having these feelings of high self-esteem. In addition, most of us have a need for recognition from others, the need for praise, and the need to feel that we are valued by others.

Self-Actualization

The need for self-actualization is the desire to become more and more what one is, to become everything that one is capable of becoming. People at this level of need-fulfillment seek knowledge, peace, esthetic experiences, self-fulfillment, meaning, and spirituality.

Now, for the practice: Fill in the missing Maslow need based on the angry expression.

> *Most humans have a desire to belong to groups, to feel loved by others, and to be accepted by others. Once we feel secure, and safe, according to Maslow, we are motivated to satisfy our love and belongingness needs.*

Angry Expression #1:

"You work all the time and are never with the family"

Expectation: To spend more time with the family

Feeling/Emotion: Anger, frustration

Underlying Need: _____

Angry Expression #2:

"All you ever do is criticize me."

Expectation: To be seen positively by partner

Feeling/Emotion: Disrespected, inferior, inadequate

Underlying Need: _____

Angry Expression #4:
"Why can't you ever get dinner ready on time?"

Expectation: Regular meal hours

Feeling/Emotion: Frustrated, hungry, irritated

Underlying Need: _____

Angry Expression #5:
"You lied to me about the checkbook"

Expectation: Honesty in relationship

Feeling/Emotion: Angry, scared, embarrassed

Underlying Need: _____

Angry Expression #6:
"Why can't you accept that I have to spend so much time volunteering at the Assistance League?"

Expectation: For your partner to understand your need for time to volunteer.

Feeling/Emotion: Not understood, angry, controlled, trapped

Underlying Need: _____

> *Some people have a very high need for security in almost every aspect of their lives, while other people have a much lower need for safety; for them, excitement, adventure, or risk is much more important.*

Finding Other Ways To Satisfy Your Needs

Communicating clearly what your needs are is a powerful tool for anger management and improving your relationships. But, now the bad news—certain important people in your life are incapable, uninterested, or unwilling to meet some of your needs. In this case, you may want to explore and find alternative ways to get what you need, rather than being constantly upset with those who aren't doing what they "should."

www.centuryangermanagement.com / Copyright 2005

> *We all have needs, contrary to some popular thinking; it is not selfish to recognize and try to get our needs fulfilled.*

Why, for example, does your partner have to love boating as much as you do? If you get angry because she does not share your sailing enthusiasm, perhaps you could consider joining a sailing club and enjoy some Sunday afternoons with other sailors—making sure, of course, that you negotiate equal time with her.

As another example, you may be angry because you basically dislike aspects of your job, but for economic or practical reasons, you cannot quit at this time even though you are feeling dissatisfied and unfulfilled. Why not get your needs met with hobbies, an avocation, or a "moonlight" job? You might even consider a volunteer position of some kind that makes you feel good about yourself and your life, and improves your self-esteem.

Finding alternative ways to become a happier and less angry person is a journey in self-development that begins by taking responsibility for your own needs and finding workable and acceptable ways of satisfying those needs.

NOTES

Anger Control Tool #7
Forgive, But Don't Forget

In the long run, it's not a question of whether they deserve to be forgiven. You're not forgiving them for their sake. You're doing it for yourself.

"In the long run, it's not a question of whether they deserve to be forgiven. You're not forgiving them for their sake. You're doing it for yourself. For your own health and well-being, forgiveness is simply the most energy-efficient option. It frees you from the incredibly toxic, debilitating drain of holding a grudge. Don't let these people live rent free in your head. If they hurt you before, why let them keep doing it year after year in your mind? It's not worth it, but it takes heart effort to stop it. You can muster that heart power to forgive them as a way of looking out for yourself. It's one thing you can be totally selfish about."

— Doc Childre and Howard Martin, The HeartMath Solution

We sometimes ask our clients if they have or currently hold a grudge towards someone else. Inevitably, there is always someone that says, "I do!" Then we ask how often they think about that person and the feelings they have when they think about them. Although the frequency of the thoughts varies, the feelings are universal. Clients say things like, "I get really angry, upset, and irritated when I think about _____". It takes a lot of mental energy to hold a grudge and these negative feelings occupy precious and useful space in our minds. We always ask clients what it would be like to replace this negative space with positive feelings. Unanimously, they cheer, "That would be terrific!" Holding a grudge is a choice, and it's up to you to decide if you want to fill valuable space in your heart and mind with negative or positive thoughts.

> *Each of us has experienced hurt brought on by remarks made or deeds done by friends, family, coworkers, neighbors or other people in our lives. If we respond skillfully, we can shake it off or otherwise deal with the hurt in a way that does not affect our lives for long.*

Each of us has experienced hurt brought on by remarks made or deeds done by friends, family members, coworkers, neighbors or other people in our lives. If we respond skillfully, we can shake it off or otherwise deal with the hurt in a way that does not affect our lives for long. However, sometimes we don't deal with it well, resulting in developing a "grievance" toward that person or situation.

Put another way, grievances are formed when we are unable to deal successfully when we don't get what we want or deserve and then we dwell on the injustice in our minds. By contrast, forgiveness is the process of healing that grievance so we can live with the injustice in a peaceful way.

The following are some common examples of situations and people struggling with grievances ranging from the trivial to catastrophic. Put yourself in their situation and see if you can notice how quickly the people progress from feelings of hurt and anger to forming a bona-fid grievance.

• Jim was in a relationship for one year. One day his partner announces she wants to end it. Jim is devastated and starts telling himself how she has taken advantage of him, ruined his life and made a fool of him. He could not concentrate at work and spent his time repeating his story to whoever would listen.

• Mary's business partner leaves the partnership without notice or forwarding address and Mary was left holding the business and the debts alone. She was bitter and angry. One year later, Mary filed bankruptcy due to her crushing debt and inability to let go of the emotional resentment she feels toward her prior partner and what he did to her.

• Nancy is a single parent to an adult child living with her in an apartment. Her daughter was careless and left the keys in her only automobile, which they both shared. It was stolen, leaving both of them without transportation. Nancy can hardly stand to look at her daughter. She becomes extremely angry, even though her daughter has apologized and tried to make up for error.

• Betsy's mother was an alcoholic, which deprived her of a normal childhood, including not being able to get an adequate education. Betsy has suffered and had to take low-paying jobs as a result. Her mother, now sober, wants a new relationship with her, but she avoids her mother and the issue by putting up an emotional wall between the two of them.

> ## *If we have certain personality traits or a certain type of background we might even convince ourselves that bad things happen to us more frequently than to other people.*

• Stacy's partner of twelve years does not come home one evening and she knew he was with a former lover. He begged for another chance with Stacy, but her pride and anger held her back. Stacy said she would feel like a fool if she forgave him, even though she still loved him. Stacy didn't end the relationship, but reminds him daily of what he did to her.

In each of these examples, the "hurt" wasn't dealt with in a healthy way and led to the formation of "grievance." How this occurs has been studied by Dr. Fred Luskin, the Director and Founder of the Stanford University Forgiveness Project. According to his studies, three steps are involved when you develop a grievance:

• You take the offense too personally.

• You blame the offender for how you feel.

• You create a grievance story.

Taking the Offense Too Personally

When an offense occurs, when we feel emotional pain, or when something bad happens to us, it is natural to say to yourself, "Why Me?" "Why am I the only one?" "Why was I singled out?" If we have certain personality traits or a certain type of background we might even convince ourselves that bad things happen to us more frequently than to other people. Locking ourselves into this kind of thinking puts us on the road to forming a grievance because it means we are focusing on the event in a way to make it personal for us, when in reality, most events have both personal and impersonal elements to them.

As an alternative, we should try to see *both* the personal and the impersonal nature of our hurt—to see that many lovers leave their partners, that thousands of children grow up in alcoholic homes, and that untold numbers of business partnership fail because of the actions of one of the partners that wasn't anticipated when the partnership was formed. Remembering how common your suffering is in no way is meant to make it seem trivial or unimportant, but seeing the broader picture is an important healing tool to reduce your pain and resentment toward what happened to you.

A second way to take the offense less personally is to realize that most offenses are committed without the intention of hurting anyone personally. Nancy's daughter did not intend on complicating her mother's life by accidentally leaving the keys in the car. Jim's partner did not leave him with the intent of hurting him—only to move on to another relationship that she thought would work better for her. Betsy's mother did not become an alcoholic with the intent of destroying her daughter's life.

Taking things less personally does not mean that we have to like what was done to us or that we deny the impact on us. But, finding a way to see both the personal and impersonal aspects of your grievance is the first step in your healing process.

Blaming the Offender for How You Feel

Thirty-two year old Elizabeth cried during her anger management class as she related how one year ago her 19-month old girl was permanently brain-damaged as the result of medical error at the hospital in which she was delivered. She definitely has a legitimate grievance toward the hospital and the medical staff and felt that she could never forgive them for what she saw as their incompetence. She clearly was not yet ready to forgive and she needed her simmering anger to motivate her to do what she felt she needed to do legally and otherwise to deal with this horrific situation.

Yet even in this tragic situation, at some point in the future when she is ready, Elizabeth might elect to find a way to forgive. For her to be able to do this, after a certain amount of time, she will have to take the step of separating in her mind two things: (1) blaming the hospital for what they did and (2) blaming them for her resulting feelings about the situation. Elizabeth cannot change what was done to her daughter, but she can change her current feelings about it and she can change how she lives the rest of her life. If she continues to hold an intense grievance, she is giving all the power to what happened in the past to determine her present emotional well being—almost like being victimized again while remaining in her emotional prison.

No one lights the path to this kind of thinking more than psychiatrist Dr. Victor Frankl who was a victim of the Nazis and experienced the horrors of the Holocaust firsthand. Dr. Frankl does not believe that people should accept injustice, but that we should fight evil and victimization in all ways possible. But, he also recognized that while no one can change the past, they can change their attitudes and feelings toward their injustice and suffering by finding meaning in what happened and somehow integrating that meaning into the larger context of one's life.

He encourages victims to ask themselves, "Did I learn anything from your unjust experience?" "Did it make me a stronger person, a more sensitive person, a person who is more mature, courageous or more

> *Taking things less personally does not mean that we have to like what was done to us or that we deny the impact on us. But, finding a way to seeing both the personal and impersonal aspects of your grievance is the first step in your healing process.*

peaceful?" "Did others somehow gain because of what I endured and how I matured?"

Viewed this way, Elizabeth began to feel a little better about her situation and allowed that indeed her daughter had been making progress, that now she learned to notice the little things about her daughter's development that brought her great joy, and taking care of her daughter now defined her life's purpose. While Elizabeth's journey of forgiveness is still a long one, she has taken the first step in finding some meaning in the tragedy that occurred. Perhaps, as someone once said, the best revenge is doing well after being victimized.

Creating a Grievance Story

As children grow past their second birthdays, storytelling becomes a vital form of communicating with other children and adults. Storytelling is also vital for children to understand themselves and their lives. It helps us all make sense of our lives and of other people. Stories enable us to understand the complex social worlds in which we all live.

People ask us, "How did you become a lawyer, or a doctor, or an air conditioning repair man?" or "How did you catch that big fish?" We have a story about how that happened. Likewise, new friends ask of you, "How did you meet your partner?" or "What caused your divorce?" Again, there is a story behind it that may change slightly or considerably as the years go by.

In a similar manner, when someone hurts us it is natural to develop a story about it that we repeat to others and ourselves. Soon the story becomes part of our grievance and becomes embedded in our minds as absolute "fact." But, there are two problems with this—both of which might cause you to think differently about your story.

The first problem is that the research shows that the story you tell about your hurt changes according to whether you were the offender or the offended, and also is influenced greatly by your past personal experiences and memories.

The second problem is that although your story may certainly be true, you may be telling it in a way to yourself and to others that hurts you more than it helps you. There are numerous ways to interpret life events: why not pick the interpretation that is most beneficial to your well being and emotional healing?

To illustrate how our grievance story can either prolong hurt or start the healing process, let's revisit several of our case examples. Nancy's

> ## *When someone hurts us it is natural to develop a story about it that we repeat to others and ourselves.*

> *It is crucial to change your grievance story as part of your process of forgiveness and achieving inner peace.*

story to her friends about her irresponsible adult daughter left out the part that she herself frequently leaves the keys in the car (which is where her daughter learned to do the same thing). Changing this to something like *"this experience taught us that we both have to learn to protect ourselves better—which we will do in the future"* would be helpful.

As another example, Stacy's story left out the part that she herself had numerous affairs. Not that two wrongs make a right, but a better story to tell herself might have been something like *"there is something fundamentally wrong in our relationship if we both feel the need to be unfaithful. Let's stop blaming each other and instead discover what it is."*

As these examples illustrate, most grievance stories are based on our tale of helplessness and frustration because of what another person or situation did to us. The grievance story seems true every time we tell it because our mind wants to accept our version of things. But, if we are not careful, our grievance story can lock us into continuing hurt, pain, and helplessness and prevent us from moving forward in our lives.

Our grievance stories not only affect us, but also our children. Recent research in neuroscience shows that the story parents have about their own lives can greatly affect how securely their children will grow up. Even if parents have had much trauma in their own lives, *how they see themselves as having dealt with it* has more to do with the emotional connection and bonding they have with their own children than does the fact of having had the trauma. The positive effects of this more secure bonding and attachment lasts a lifetime for their children.

For all these reasons, it is crucial to change your grievance story as part of your process of forgiveness and achieving inner peace. The trick is to amend it so that you are a hero or survivor of your trauma rather than a victim of it. Develop a story that shows how you overcame difficulty or became a better person, or benefited in the long run from what happened to you.

Remember Mary whose business partner left her with staggering debt and obligation, resulting in a forced bankruptcy filing? She developed the following story, which empowered her to reconstruct her life:

Five years ago, I thought I was on top of the world. I had a good business going, I had good money coming in and the future looked bright. When my partner bailed without telling me, I was temporarily devastated. I became extremely depressed, and shamed because I had to file bankruptcy. Even worse, this happened at the exact age that my mother's business failed, so I convinced myself that this was a weird "kismet"—that I was recreating history or somehow playing out our family fate. After feeling sorry for myself for several months, I finally decided "enough" – that I wasn't going to let my partner's defection destroy my business career.

To beef-up my business skills, so I could rely on my own judgment rather than someone else's, I enrolled in a business school in which I took a class that gave me a great concept for a brand new business. This new business concept changed my life. I later learned that many successful people have several bankruptcies in their past. This helped me get past my shame. In a way, my old partner did me a favor by forcing me to take a good look at myself, get more skills, and grow as a person. I now like myself again and now I'm able to see that what happened to me was a painful, expensive, and traumatic experience, but in the long run a valuable life lesson.

Should You Forgive?

Should you always forgive? The answer to this question always comes down to personal choices and decisions. Some people in our anger management classes feel that certain things cannot and shouldn't be forgiven while other participants feel that ultimately anything can be forgiven. As an example of what is possible in terms of forgiveness, the staff of the Stanford Forgiveness Project successfully worked with Protestant and Catholic families of Northern Ireland whose children had been killed by each others' families.

On the other hand, Dr. Abrams-Spring, who wrote a classic book called *After the Affair*, cautions that forgiving a cheating partner too quickly or too easily can be an indication of your low self-esteem. She maintains that forgiveness must be earned by the offending partner and not given automatically.

Deciding if you should forgive or not may be easier after reviewing exactly what forgiveness is and what it is not.

- ***Forgiving does not mean that you forget the offense.*** You may never forget (and probably shouldn't) what happened to you, but after forgiveness you can remember it without the emotional pain connected to it.

- ***Forgiving does not mean that you are saying what they did was okay.*** Quite the opposite. We can forgive, but still see what happened to you as horrific or unjust.

- ***You don't need to even tell people that you forgive them; the forgiveness occurs in your heart, not in conversation with them. Although in some circumstances, you may want to have a dialogue***

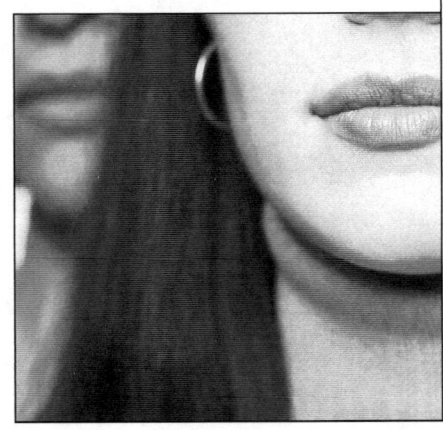

> **Should you always forgive? The answer to this question always comes down to personal choices and decisions.**

> **Forgiveness and trust are two separate issues. Even after forgiveness, it may take a long time to re-build trust, if ever.**

about it. It often backfires if you go up to someone (especially a relative) and say "I forgive you." This occurs because the offending person often doesn't see himself or herself as the problem. Better to do the forgiveness in your own mind and heart. One exception to this is if you are the victim of a violent crime. Some studies show that it helps your healing if you forgive your assailant face to face.

- *Forgiving doesn't mean you will automatically trust them again.* Forgiveness and trust are two separate issues. Even after forgiveness, it may take a long time to re-build trust, if ever. To instantly trust someone again after they have violated you in some way is not a sign of good mental health or strong self-esteem.

- *Forgiving doesn't necessary mean you like or love the offender, or even want to be in a future relationship with them.* Absence of angry feelings doesn't necessarily create warm, positive, or loving feelings in you for the offender. At best, forgiving may bring you up to neutral in your feelings toward them. It is possible to say to yourself, for instance, "Okay, I forgive her but I don't want to have anything further to do with her—ever."

- *You don't need to forgive all at once.* This is a concept that especially applies to forgiving an unfaithful partner. Dr. Abrams-Spring suggests that to start maybe you can only forgive 10%—just open the door—and then see how your unfaithful partner behaves. After a period of time, you might want to open the door a little wider and forgive maybe another 20%, and so on.

Forgiving Is Good For Your Health

Considerable medical and psychological research shows that there are benefits to both your physical health and your mental well being to forgive.

Let's start with your physical health. According to Dr. Luskin at the Stanford University Forgiveness Project, studies reveal that:

- People who are forgiving report fewer health problems.

- People who blame other people for their troubles have a higher incidence of illness such as cardiovascular disease and cancers.

- People who just imagine forgiving their offender have immediate improvements in their cardiovascular, muscular, and nervous systems.

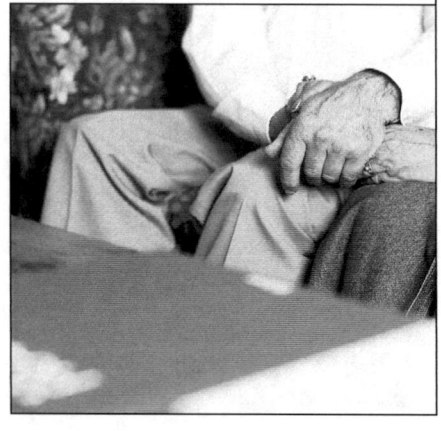

Forgiveness is a process that takes time and patience to complete.

Forgiving is Good for Your Peace of Mind

Scientific research shows that forgiveness often improves your peace of mind:

- One study done in 1996 showed that the more people forgave those who deeply hurt them, the less angry they were.

- Two studies of divorced people showed that those who forgave the former spouse were more emotionally healthy than those who chose not to forgive. The forgivers had a higher sense of well-being and lower anxiety and depression.

- Even if your spouse cheated on you, if you are able to forgive and find meaning in your suffering, you are more likely to have higher well-being and lower anxiety than those who do not forgive.

Seven Steps to Forgiveness

Forgiveness is a process that takes time and patience to complete. The following recommended steps are based on the work of the Stanford Forgiveness Project and the feedback given to us by anger management participants who were learning to forgive:

Step 1 – Write down your grievance or issue that you would like to forgive

_____

_____

_____

Step 2 – Make a decision and a commitment to forgive.

You must be ready for this step, remembering that forgiveness is for you and not for anyone else. No one else even needs to know about your decision

☐   I make a commitment to start the forgiveness process

☐   Honestly, I am not yet ready.

Step 3 – Write down your goal of forgiveness, remembering that forgiveness does not necessarily mean reconciling with the person who upset you.

Remember also that by forgiving it does not mean you are condoning their actions or what they did to you.

My goal in forgiving is _____

_____

_____

_____

_____

Step 4 – Recognize that forgiveness can be defined as the peace and understanding that comes from blaming less that which has hurt you, taking the experience less personally, and changing your grievance story.

I could take what happened to me less personally by remembering the following _____

_____

_____

_____

I could change my grievance story in the following way to remind myself that I have the heroic choice to forgive:

_____

_____

_____

_____

_____

_____

_____

> *Remember also that by forgiving it does not mean you are condoning their actions or what they did to you.*

> *While you may have to think about it awhile, ask yourself what it is that you really want to achieve that your grievance is interfering with or preventing you from having.*

Step 5 – Commit to relaxing and soothing yourself whenever you start getting upset upon thinking of your grievance.

We have given you numerous exercises to do this in other parts of this program. Pick one of the following that works for you:

☐ **Counting Breaths – p. 14**

☐ **Letting Go of Tension – p. 14**

☐ **Freeze-Frame Technique – p. 96**

Step 6 - List your "positive intentions"

This involves focusing on other ways to get your positive goals met rather than through the experience that has hurt you. Grievances may derail us—throw us off course —causing us to lose motivation to keep pursing what we want and what is important to us.

To illustrate how this works, let's re-visit the case of Betsy who resented her alcoholic mother for depriving her of numerous life opportunities. Eventually, Betsy was able to see that she did not have to give up her aspirations or goals because of what happened to her as a child. Why couldn't she still pursue her lifetime ambition of helping other people by becoming a nurse or a therapist? There are many ways to do this without early family support if education is viewed as a lifelong process. Once Betsy remembered what she really wanted out of life, she was able to figure out a way to get it; she enrolled in community college and was recently accepted into a 4-year RN program. Once her life was on track, she was able start the process of forgiveness and discovered many admirable and likable traits in her now sober and functioning mother.

While you may have to think about it awhile, ask yourself what it is that you really want to achieve that your grievance is interfering with or preventing you from having.

My positive intentions (goals) around my grievances are:

_____

_____

_____

_____

_____

Now that I think about it, how else might I achieve these goals or get my needs met?

_____

_____

_____

_____

_____

> *Remember that a life well lived is your best revenge. Instead of focusing on your hurt and pain, learn to look for the positives in your life.*

Step 7- Refocus on positives in your life

Remember that a life well lived is your best revenge. Instead of focusing on your hurt and pain (which gives the person who hurt you power over you), learn to look for the positives in your life. If you look hard enough, you will find many things in your life to be grateful for. We recall an elderly lady we knew in a nursing home who always managed to have a positive attitude toward things. Curious, we asked her how she would define "a good day." Her reply: "It is a good day if I wake up with the grass *under* my feet." Now, that is perspective!

People who find a way to see love, beauty, and kindness around them are better able to forgive and get past their life grievances. Remember, your world is filled with positives and negatives, love and hatred, beauty and ugliness, pain and joy, kindness and cruelty. It is up to you to decide what to focus on.

The positives in my life now that I can focus on more are:

_____

_____

_____

_____

_____

_____

_____

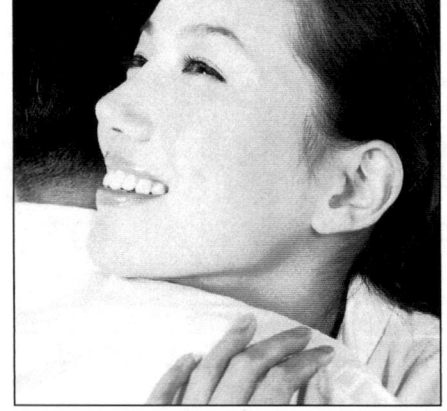

www.centuryangermanagement.com / Copyright 2005

NOTES

_____

_____

_____

_____

_____

_____

_____

_____

_____

_____

_____

_____

_____

_____

_____

_____

_____

_____

_____

_____

_____

_____

_____

NOTES

Anger Control Tool #8
Retreat and Think Things Over

> *Learning to retreat and think things over is a skill that will reap great benefits to you and those around you because it will help keep you in the problem-solving stage of conflict resolution and keep things from getting out of hand.*

Jim and Mary Jones loved each other deeply, but often got into horrific verbal battles over any number of issues. They would argue and yell for hours, often into the night, leaving both of them exhausted, emotionally disconnected, hurt, and resentful toward each other because of all the unfair, untrue, distorted, and mean-spirited things said during the never-ending arguments. Both became so upset they were flooded with negative feelings that prevented their being able to repair the damage, to think rationally, or to problem-solve the issues at hand. The longer they argued, the worse things became and the more their issues escalated until there basically was no hope of resolving things at that point. The end result was days of "silent treatment" toward each other, very hurt feelings, and miles of emotional distance between them.

Much of this emotional suffering could have been prevented or at least minimized had they learned to "Retreat and Think Things Over." Basically, this means to temporarily distance yourself from each other for a period of time so that both of you can calm down. This allows your bodily systems to return to normal, and allows your normally good reasoning and thinking ability to return.

You may be thinking, "Easier said than done!" Yes, that is true because this is one of those tools that sounds deceptively simple, yet it is by no means easy to do for at least two reasons.

First, there is a common myth among many of us that all relationship conflicts should be "settled" in the moment while the intense feelings

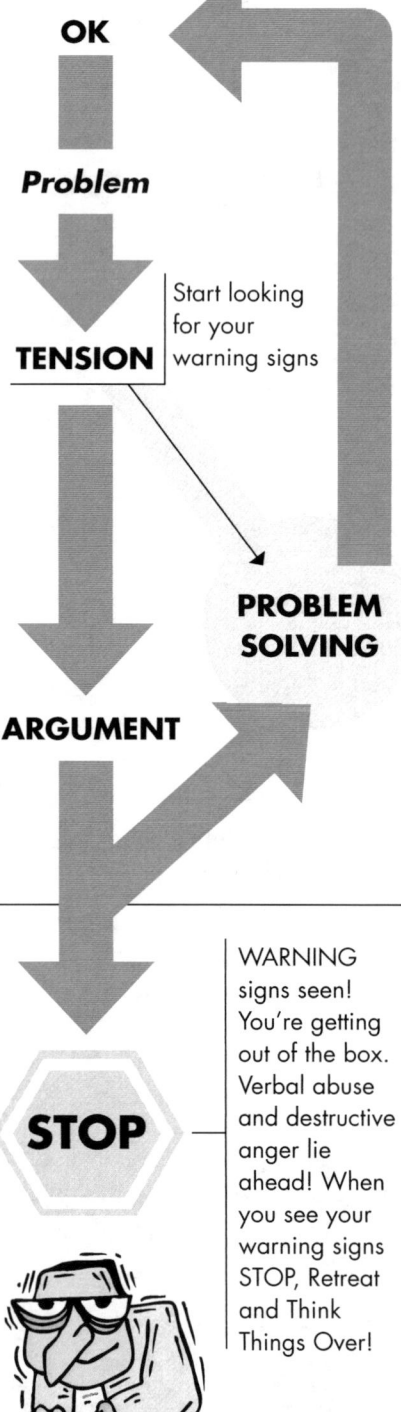

Warning Signs and Time Outs

OK

Problem

TENSION — Start looking for your warning signs

ARGUMENT

PROBLEM SOLVING

STOP — WARNING signs seen! You're getting out of the box. Verbal abuse and destructive anger lie ahead! When you see your warning signs STOP, Retreat and Think Things Over!

FEELING FLOODED DPA → Destructive and Angry Behavior AND/OR Emotional Disengagement

are present. If you do not do this, you may be accused of "avoiding" the issue, or "invalidating" the feelings of your partner. Hence, many couples refuse to give their partner "space" during an argument and insist on immediate discussion and resolution of the issue. Even worse, in misguided attempts to try and gain control of the situation, spouses will sometimes physically block the escape of their angry partner, or will follow them from room to room demanding discussion. This is a dangerous practice as it can escalate levels of anger even further, and cause partners to do and say things they don't really don't mean and may later regret!

A second reason this tool is challenging to use effectively is because once stress and anger levels reach a certain point, one or both partners reach a point of no-return. In effect, the "emotional brain" takes over and one or both partners feel flooded with negative feelings, making it difficult to disengage from each other and stop the fight. It is like your brain is "hijacked" from reason by all the intense emotions you are feeling.

This "hijacking" or "flooding" has been studied by the marital researchers at the Gottman Institute who call it "Diffuse Physiological Arousal" (DPA, for short). DPA can occur whenever your pulse rate exceeds 100 beats per minute (a common occurrence during marital conflict). Once in DPA, other changes occur as well: muscle tension, increase in blood pressure, decreased ability to reason, impaired memory, and decreased ability to gain perspective on a situation (your focus becomes like a laser beam, seeing only what is immediately in front of you instead of the bigger picture).

Stay In the Box

Learning to retreat and think things over is a skill that will reap great benefits to you and those around you because it will help keep you in the problem-solving stage of conflict resolution and keep things from getting out of hand. Dr. Bill Adams, director of a domestic violence counseling program in Long Beach, California, calls this process "Staying in the box."

Adapted from The Choices Program; *How to Stop Hurting The People Who Love You.*
Copyright ©2003 William E. Adams, Ph.D. Used by permission of William E. Adams, Ph.D.

> *The alternative [to retreat and think things over] is increased conflict, emotional flooding, and destructive, angry behavior —or painful emotional disengagement otherwise known as "the cold war" often experienced by troubled couples.*

To understand how the process in this diagram works, let us return to our conflicting couple, Jim and Mary. As is the case with almost all couples, once a problem starts, it turns into tension experienced by one or both of the partners. If the tension leads to problem solving or least dialog about the issue, Jim and Mary stay in the box and all is well.

In the case of Jim and Mary, however, their marital tension lead them down another path to severe arguing. Even at this point, they could have stayed in the box by finding a way to solve the issues. Unfortunately, their arguing and conflict escalated until they were clearly "out of the box."

It is at this point that it is crucial for one or both partners to *retreat and think things over*—often called "taking a time-out." Use this tool to get back into the box where it is much more likely you will resolve the issues between you. The alternative, as the diagram clearly shows, is increased conflict, emotional flooding, and destructive and angry behavior, or painful emotional disengagement, otherwise known as "the cold war," often experienced by troubled couples.

Warning Signs

What warning signs should Jim and Mary have looked for that alerted them to the fact that they were getting out of the box?

• Feeling overwhelmed during an argument.

• Raising their voice to an unusual level.

• Feeling out of control with their temper.

• Feeling so much negativity that they have difficulty focusing on their thoughts.

• Things getting out of hand quickly during discussion.

• Inability to think straight when starting to feel hostile.

• Thinking to themselves, "Why can't I talk more logically?"

• Feeling like running away during your fights.

• Small issues suddenly becoming big ones.

• Inability to calm themselves down during the argument.

• Heart racing.

• Muscles tensing.

> *Temporarily removing yourself from the situation allows your body to return to normal, provides a cooling-down time, and allows your brain to return to its normal state in which you can reason and think better.*

Why "Retreat and Thinking Things Over" Works

Temporarily removing yourself from the situation allows your body to return to normal, provides a cooling-down time, and allows your brain to return to it's normal state in which you can reason and think better. This tool also prevents you or your partner from saying unfair or hurtful things in the heat of battle, which can easily escalate into further conflicts and resentments, causing you and your partner to become even more emotionally cut off and distanced from each other.

Inside your head, your "emotional brain" is overtaking your "thinking brain" once you allow yourself to either get out of the box or stay out of the box. When this happens, your brain is taking the "low-road" to functioning—you simply are not yourself and certainly not at your best. By using the "Retreat and Think Things Over" tool effectively, you allow your brain to switch to the "high-road"— the path that allows your emotions and thoughts to be integrated and to work together, so that you can better deal with the conflict or issue at hand.

Some Basic Rules

Remember that we said the "Retreat and Think Things Over" tool is simple but not easy? What we meant was that for this tool to work effectively, you must stick to some basic rules when using it.

Rule #1
You can only use the tool for yourself, not your partner.
It does not usually work for you to tell your partner it is time for them to retreat.

Rule #2
Announce that you need to take a "Time Out and Retreat" before you do it.

This should be done using assertive communication in a way that clearly conveys your need to leave before things get out of hand, as opposed to your leaving to merely avoid dealing with the situation.

Examples 1: "Honey...I need to take a time out now because I am really worked up and afraid I will say things I don't mean."

Example 2: "I know that this issue is extremely important to you, but I just can't deal with it right now in a constructive way. I need a little time to collect myself before we discuss it further."

> *We all need support in times of crisis. And sometimes good friends or rational relatives can give us perspective and clarity, as well as that much needed understanding and sympathy when we are in crisis.*

Example 3: *"I need some time to think over what you just said. I promise to try and understand your point and we'll discuss it in a little while, OK?"*

Example 4: *(if your partner won't let you leave):* *"I know that you want to solve this right now; so do I. However, I need some space to sort things out because I just can't think straight right now. I feel confused and overwhelmed. If you let me leave, I promise we'll deal with this when I get back."*

Rule #3
You need to commit to a reasonable length of time to return and deal with the issue.

Research shows that the average person takes from 20 minutes to one hour for their bodies to return to normal after an upsetting relationship battle. If you don't commit to a specific and reasonable amount of time in returning, your partner may feel abandoned and ignored which, of course, will only make things much worse. Don't be like one husband we knew who didn't quite comply with the spirit of this tool; he came back three days later to deal with an understandably outraged wife.

Rule #4
Don't drink or use drugs during this time.

It will only make things worse and interfere with your ability to do the constructive and healing things you need to be doing during your retreat time. And of course, it will be much harder, if not impossible, to convince your partner of your sincerity in wanting to work things out if you return intoxicated or high.

Rule #5
Be very careful and very selective in who you talk to during your retreat time.

There is a natural tendency, of course, to contact a friend or sympathetic relative who you know will take your side in the dispute or conflict. We all need support in times of crisis. And sometimes good friends or rational relatives can give us perspective and clarity, as well as that much needed understanding and sympathy when we are in crisis.

But, you should be careful in discussing relationship problems with others, especially family, because they may permanently have a negative view of your partner, even after you have made up and things are now fixed in the relationship. You can't necessarily expect your family to turn the positive emotions back on like you have.

> *When flooded and overwhelmed, it helps to stop the movie—or freeze just one frame. This frame can be the conflict you had with your partner before leaving to regroup and marshal your emotional resources.*

Case example: *After a twenty-six year marriage, Kathy discovered that her husband, Fred, had been visiting a brothel in Nevada. Outraged, she downloaded pictures of actual encounters from her husband's computer and showed them to her aging and conservative Catholic parents. Needless to say, this destroyed the previously close relationship and trust the husband had with his in-laws. One year later, Kathy and her husband worked things out and decided to reconcile. However, her parents cannot accept Kathy's husband back into the family, which now is causing much pain to both Kathy and Fred.*

What to Do During Your Time-out After You Retreat

Finally, you are out of the house, but still fuming, agitated, and upset. What should you do during this time to calm down and prepare for the upcoming return to your partner? Ideally, you should remain alone and do two things:

(1) Sooth yourself to feel better, calm yourself, and gain perspective

(2) Change your internal conversation—your self-talk—to control those angry feelings.

The Freeze-frame Technique for Self-Soothing

The Institute of HeartMath has developed an excellent exercise called "freeze-frame" that is ideal for self-soothing during your retreat time. The best part is that while it only takes a couple of minutes to do it, the results can be quite astounding. The technique is based on the idea that, like movies, our conscious life is made up of a series of incidents—or frames— strung together over time. When flooded and overwhelmed, it helps to stop the movie or freeze just one frame. This frame can be the conflict you had with your partner before leaving to regroup and marshal your emotional resources.

Once you freeze this frame in your mind (you can close your eyes, or not, depending on what makes you feel comfortable), put your hand on your heart and pretend your heart is "breathing" as you inhale and exhale. Make a sincere effort to shift your focus away from your racing mind or disturbed emotions to the area around your heart.

As you relax and calm down, try recalling the feeling of a *positive time or experience you've had in your life.*

Now, using your intuition, common sense, and sincerity ask your heart what would be a better response to the situation, one that would repair the damage to your relationship. Then, *listen* to what your heart answers to your question.

> ## *It is crucial to change your self-talk before returning to your partner, or else you may find yourself more angry when you return than you were when you left.*

Don't worry if you have trouble recalling that positive time or experience; the technique will help you even if you just feel neutral —instead of positive—during this step.

Believe it or not, recent scientific research shows that the heart (and also your gut) actually may be able to do some of what your brain does in terms of giving you answers; it may be that your heart actually can function like a little satellite of the brain, and hence, may be able to give you some answers just like your brain does.

Change That Self-Talk

It is crucial to change your self-talk before returning to your partner, or else you may find yourself more angry when you return than you were when you left. This is the time to use Tool 4—changing that conversation with yourself. The following are additional self-talk phrases that may be especially helpful to you during your "Retreat and Think Things Over" time. Check those that might apply to your situation and those that would be helpful to you:

☐ I am responsible for my own anger and my own feelings.

☐ Maybe we are trying to solve an unsolvable (perpetual) problem.

☐ I need to look at my part in the conflict.

☐ Nobody is perfect. I can forgive myself for behaving badly.

☐ Nobody is perfect. I can forgive him/her for behaving badly.

☐ I must remember all the reasons I love him/her.

☐ Maybe I expect too much from others.

☐ Maybe I expect too much from myself.

☐ I need to work on seeing things from his/her point of view.

☐ My partner is doing the best she/he can.

☐ It doesn't matter who is "right"; solving the problem is the important thing.

☐ I will try to solve the problem, according to what my heart told me in "freeze-frame."

☐ Having a good relationship is more important than "winning" this issue.

☐ It is damaging to our children to witness this conflict.

> *Having a good relationship is more important than "winning" this issue.*

☐ This issue is not that important. I will pick my battles.

☐ I can decide how I will respond best to this situation.

☐ I have handled more stress than this in the past.

☐ I let myself get out of the box by ignoring my warning signs.

☐ I can repair the emotional damage I caused.

☐ I will try a "softer" startup to get a discussion going when I get back.

☐ Maybe we can find a compromise for the problem.

www.centuryangermanagement.com / Copyright 2005

NOTES

NOTES

_____

_____

_____

_____

_____

_____

_____

_____

_____

_____

_____

_____

_____

_____

_____

_____

_____

_____

_____

_____

_____

_____

_____

_____

_____

_____

_____

www.centuryangermanagement.com / Copyright 2005

Appendix 1

Holmes-Rahe Social Readjustment Rating Scale

This allows you to determine the total amount of stress you have been exposed to in the last year by adding up the relative stress values, known as Life Change Units (LCU), for various events. A score of 250 or more is considered high. Persons with a low stress tolerance may find themselves overstressed with a score of 150. The test is used to determine disease susceptibility. According to current research, with a score of 150 or less, you have a 30% chance of becoming seriously ill. Between 150 to 299 and it jumps to 50%. Over 300 and there's an 80% chance of serious illness in the next 2 years. Because some of this research is controversial, it is best to use these numbers as guidelines only. And remember, it is not only events that stress us—it is our ability to cope that determines the effect any particular stressor will have on us.

Reprinted (with minor variations) from Journal of Psychosomatic Research, VII:214, Thomas Holms and Richard Rahe, "Holmes-Rahe Social Readjustment Scale," 213-218, 1967, with permission from Elsevier.

Adult Stressor:

Check if event has occurred in the last year

	Event	Value
☐	Death of spouse	100
☐	Divorce	73
☐	Separation from living partner	65
☐	Jail term or probation	63
☐	Death of close family member other than spouse	63
☐	Serious personal injury or illness	53
☐	Marriage	50
☐	Fired at work	47
☐	Marital reconciliation	40
☐	Retirement	45
☐	Change in health of immediate family member	44
☐	Pregnancy	40
☐	Sex difficulties	39
☐	Gain of new family member	39
☐	Business readjustment	39

	Event	Value
☐	Change in financial state	38
☐	Death of a close friend	37
☐	Change in number of arguments with spouse	35
☐	Mortgage or loan for a major purpose	30
☐	Foreclosure of mortgage or loan	30
☐	Trouble with in-laws	29
☐	Change in responsibilities at work	29
☐	Son or daughter leaving home	29
☐	Outstanding personal achievement	28
☐	Spouse begins or stops work	26
☐	Begin or end school	26
☐	Change in living conditions	25
☐	Revision in personal habits	24
☐	Trouble with boss	23
☐	Change in work hours or conditions	20
☐	Change in residence	20
☐	Change in schools	20
☐	Change in recreation	19
☐	Major change in church activities	19
☐	Change in social activities (more or less than before)	18
☐	Mortgage or financial loan less than $30,000	17
☐	Change in sleeping habits	16
☐	Change in frequency of family get-togethers	15
☐	Change in eating habits	15
☐	Vacation	13
☐	Christmas alone	12
☐	Minor violation of the law	11

www.centuryangermanagement.com / Copyright 2005

Appendix 2

Personal Anger Record: The SERA Process

This is an ongoing record of how you have handled angry feelings since starting your anger management class. It is very important for you to keep track of events in this record so you can see patterns in your anger problem and so you can chart your progress from week to week.

Date _____   Time _____

Incident that triggered angry feelings involved:

☐ Partner or Relationship

☐ Co-Worker

☐ Boss, Supervisor, or Manager

☐ Child

☐ Parent

☐ Stranger

☐ Other

Briefly describe what happened _____

_____

_____

_____

_____

_____

S = Self-Talk
What self-talk were you having as a result of the incident?

_____

_____

_____

_____

_____

E = Emotions

What emotions or feelings were you having? (check all that apply)

☐ Anger

☐ Frustration

☐ Rage

☐ Fear

☐ Contempt

☐ Resentment

☐ Irritation

☐ Other _____

R = Response

How did you respond to the incident? What did you do?

_____

_____

_____

How do you feel you handled it?

☐ Very poorly

☐ Could have done better

☐ Very well–it was a victory!

A = Alternative

Which of the 8 anger control tools should you have used that would have helped?

☐ Stress management

☐ Empathy

☐ Assertive communication

☐ Self-talk

☐ Adjust expectations

☐ Acceptance/forgiveness

☐ Time-out

☐ Respond instead of react

References and Resources for More Information

Introduction

On understanding anger as a normal emotion, see essay by the American Psychological Association on the web at: **http://www.apa.org/pubinfo/anger.html**

On emotions, structures of the brain, how the brain works, and emotional regulation, see Daniel J Siegel, M. D., *The Developing Mind* (New York: The Guilford Press, 1999).

On the negative effects of family violence and conflict on the mental health of teens, see Jenkins, J. *Child Development*, January 2005; vol 76: pp 24-39.; on the devastating effects of extreme conflict on the home on young children, see a report by The National Research Council, *Understanding Violence Against Women* (Washington: National Academy Press, 1996, p. 74-80).

On the negative effects of anger on your health see *"Can a Troubled mind spell trouble for the heart? Part 1.* Harvard Mental Health Newsletter, Vol. 19, No. 10, April 2003; *Anger Management Improves Heart Health,* Archives of Internal Medicine, 2002, 162: 901-906; Elaine D. Eaker, ScD, et.al., *Anger and Hostility Predict the Development of Atrial Fibrillation in Men in the Framingham Offspring Study,* Circulation, 2004, 109: 1267-1271.

Tool #1– Dealing With Stress

Much of the work in this chapter is based on the work of Dr. Bruce McEwen, an internationally recognized authority. He advocates that while some stress is inevitable, being "stressed-out" isn't. In his book, he recommends ways to learn to re-channel the powerful stress activators in our lives to make us more resilient. See Bruce S. McEwen, *The End Of Stress As We Know It,* (Washington: Joseph Henry Press, 2001)

On workplace stress, an authoritative resource is *The National Institute for Occupational Safety and Health (NIOSH).* The document used for this chapter was a booklet called *Stress... At Work.* This booklet highlights the causes of stress at work and outlines steps that can be taken to prevent job-related stress. It can be downloaded from the internet in either HTML or pdf format at:

http://www.cdc.gov/niosh/atwork.html
For an excellent resource exploring whether or not coping with chronic problems differs in form, emphasis, or function from the ways people handle acute life events and transitions, see Benjamin H. Gottlieb, *Coping with Chronic Stress,* (Philadelphia: Kluwer Academic Publishers, 1997).

On the beneficial effects of relaxation and meditation, from lowered blood pressure to a reducation in heart disease, based on studies at Boston's Beth-Israel Hospital and Harvard Medical School, see Herbert Benson, M.D., *The Relaxation Response,* (New York: Perennial Currents, 2000); see also Dr. Jon-Kabat-Zinn, *Mindful Meditation – Cultivate Mindfullness-Enrich your Life.* Description and CD purchase at:
http://www.nightingale.com/tproducts_productdetailasp?product idn=12330

Another excellent resource on all aspects of stress is *The American Association of Stress.*

For a general discussion of stress, visit:
http://www.stress.org

For stress and hypertension, visit:
http://www.stress.org Hypertension.htm

For statistics and information on job stress, go to:
http://www.stress.org/job.htm

For stress, type A personality, and coronary disease, visit:
http://www.stress.org/TypeA.htm

Tool #2 – Develop Empathy

For an excellent discussion and overview of the role of emotions in our lives, the following works are recommended: Daniel Goleman (narrator), *Destructive Emotions: A Scientific Dialogue with the Dalai Lama,* (New York: Bantam Dell, 2003). Daniel Goleman, (Editor), *Healing Emotions* (Boston: Shambhala Publications, 1997).

For a perspective on emotions and empathy from a neuroscientist and therapist, especially as they relate to the developing child, see Daniel J. Siegel, M. D., *The Developing Mind* (New York: The Guilford Press, 1999).

A renowned expert in nonverbal communication, Paul Ekman led a revolution in our scientific understanding of emotions. In *Emotions Revealed,* he provides a comprehensive look at the evolutionary roots of human emotions, including anger, sadness, fear, disgust, and happiness. See Paul Ekman, *Emotions Revealed,* (Bellingham, WA: Owl Press, 2004); Also see Paul Ekman, *Telling Lies: Clues to Deceit in the Marketplace, Politics, and Marriage* (New York: Norton, 1995); Fritz Strack, *Inhibiting and Facilitating Conditions of the Human Smile: A Nonobtrusive test of the Facial Feedback Hypothesis,* Journal of Personality and Social Psychology 54, no.5 (1988):768-777; and Paul Ekman and Wallace V. Friesen, *Facial Action Coding System, parts 1 and 2* (San Francisco: Human Interaction Laboratory, Dept. of Psychiatry, University of California, 1978)

On the topic of Emotional Intelligence, or "EQ," an excellent internet resource is **http: www.7seconds.org;** also see a PBS video *Emotional Intelligence with Daniel Goleman,* (PBS Home Video, a Department of the Public Broadcasting Service: Washington, D.C.,1999)

For a professional discussion of empathy, describing the basics of empathy and empathic communciation and their importance in numerous therapeutic orientations, see Richard G. Erskine, Janet P. Moursund and Rebecca L. Trautmann, *A Therapy of Contact-in Relationships,* (Boca Raton, FL: Taylor & Francis Group, 1999)

On the issue of parenting to raise more empathic and emotionally intelligent children, see John Gottman, Ph.D., *Raising An Emotionally Intelligent Child* (New York: Fireside, 1997).

Tool #3 – Respond Instead of React

On flexibility being a sign of good mental health and on neuroscience research showing that the brain is constantly searching for signals from our body and then creating emotions, see Daniel J. Siegel, M.D., *"An Interpsersonal Newurobiology of Psychotherapy: The Developing Mind and the Resolution of Trauma,"* In *Healing Trauma,* Marion Solomon and Daniel J Siegel (Eds)(New York: WW Norton, 2002)

On the issue of looking at your attitude to regulate your emotions, see Doc Childre and Howard Martin, *The HeartMath Solution* (New York: Harper Collins, 1999).

On being your own best friend to regulate your emotions, see Dr. David Burns, *Feeling Good - The New Mood Therapy* (New York: Harper Collins, 1980).

On the medical benefits of listening with your heart, see Thomas Lewis, M.D., Fari Amini, M.D., and Richard Lewis, M.D., *The General Theory of Love* (New York: Vintage Books, 2001).

For a general discussion of responding instead of reacting, see Dave Ellis and Stan Lankowitz, *Human Being – A Manual for Happiness, Health, Love, and Wealth* (Rapid City, SD, Breakthrough Enterprises, 1995).

On the issue of how different choices can lead to more happiness by nurturing traits we already possess, see Martin E. P. Seligman, Ph.D., *Authentic Happiness* (New York: Free Press, 2002).

On a fascinating discussion of how we think without thinking and make choices that seem to be made in an instant, See Malcolm Gladwell, *Blink* (New York: Little, Brown and Company, 2005).

Tool #4 – Change That Conversation With Yourself

On the ABCD model of anger control, see Bill Borcherdt, ACSW, BCD, *You Can Control Your Anger* (Sarasota, Florida, Professional Resources Press, 2000); Albert Ellis and Robert Harper, *A New Guide To Rational Living* (N. Hollywood, California: Wilshire Book Company, 1975); Albrt Ellis and R. C. Tafrate, *How To Control Your Anger Before it Controls You* (Secaucus, N. J.: Carol Publishing, 1998)

On optimistic thinking, see Martin E. P. Seligman, Ph.D., *Learned Optimism* (New York: Free Press, 1990, 1998); Martin E. P. Seligman, Ph.D., *The Optimistic Child* (New York: HarperCollins Books, 1995).

The Self-Talk Solution is a wonderful resource. This valuable book contains detailed explanations of the self-talk techniques and their effectiveness in achieving personal improvement goals. Also included are more than 2,500 personal self-talk phrases for wide variety of self-improvement goals, such as controlling your emotions, improving your sleep, setting and reaching goals, having a successful marriage, taking responsibility for your self, and more. See Shad Helmstetter, The *Self-Talk Solution,* (Boca Raton, FL: William Morrow & Co, 1987)

Tool #5 – Assertive Communication

On the harmful communication patterns of "stonewalling" criticism, defensiveness, and contempt, see John Gottman, Ph.D., *The Seven Principals For Making Marriage Work* (New York: Random House, 1999). You can also visit his website for further information at: **http://www.gottman.com**

On the "magical formula" for assertive communication, see a 20 minute video by the Hazleden Foundation, *The Art Of Assertiveness*, 15251 Pleasant Valley Road, P.O. Box 176, Center City, MN., 55012-0176. Call toll-free for information or ordering 800-328-9000.

On giving and taking praise in the workplace, see James M. Kouzes, *Encouraging The Heart* (San Fransico: Jossey-Bass, 1999)

On viewpoints toward our spouse, see S. Murray, J. Holmes, D. Dolderman and D. Griffin, "What The Motivated Mind Sees: Comparing friends' perspectives to married partners' views of each other," *Journal of Experimental Social Psychology,* 36, (2000) 600-620.

On resolving conflicts in the workplace, see Lawrence D. Schwimmer. *The Art of Resolving Conflicts in the Workplace Study Guide/Workbook.* Can be purchased from Kontola Productions, LLC., Phone: 800-989-8273. Email: **info@kantola.com**

On different styles of communication see the University of Wisconson's counseling center's website. **http://www.uwec.edu/counsel/pubs/assertivecommunication.htm**

See "The Assertive Workbook" for a self-directed program that teaches readers to speak up and say what they mean at work and at home. Written supportively, it uses proven cognitive behavioral techniques to help individuals build self-confidence, set boundaries, and determine appropriate responses. Randy J. Paterson, *The Assertiveness Workbook: How to Express Your Ideas and Stand Up for Yourself at Work and in Relationships* (Oakland, CA: New Harbinger Publications, 2000)

Tool #6 – Adjust Those Expectations

On relationship limitations, see John Gottman, *The Seven Principals For Making Marriage Work* (New York: Random House, 1999).

On the issue of being dead wrong about a remembered event, see Elizabeth F. Loftus & William H. Calvin, "Memory's Future," *Psychology Today* 34(2):55ff (March-April, 2001). This can also be read on the internet at: **http://faculty.washington.edu/eloftus/MemoryFuture.htm**
On Maslow's hierarchy of needs, visit: **http://web.utk.edu/~gwynne/maslow.HTM**

On adjusting flawed thinking, *Narrative Means to Therapeutic Ends* by Michael White and David Epston introduces the theory that people have adjustment difficulties because the story of their life, as created by themselves or others, does not match their lived experience or the expectations they place on themselves or others. See David Epston and

Michael White, *Narrative Means to Therapeutic Ends,* (New York, NY: W. W. Norton & Company, 1990).

Tool #7 – Forgive But Don't Forget!

On Dr. Luskin's work at the Stanford Forgiveness Project, see Fred Luskin, Ph.D., *Forgive For Good* (New York: HarperCollins, 2002). See also Robert D. Enright, Ph.D., *Forgiveness Is A Choice* (Washington, APA Lifetools, American Psychological Association, 2001),

On forgiving after an affair, see Janis Abrams Spring, Ph.D., *After The Affair* (New York: HarperCollins, 1996). Also by the same author see *How Can I Forgive You?* (New York: HarperCollins, 2004)

On the issue of forgiveness in divorce, see K. A. Ashleman, *Forgiveness as a Resiliency Factor in Divorced or Permanently Separated Families.* (Madison: University of Wisconsin, 1996); also see G. Reed, *Forgiveness as a Function of Moral Agency in the Context of Infidelity and Divorce* (Madison: University of Wisconsin, 1996).

On the issue of Dr. Frankl and forgiveness, see V. Frankl, *Man's Search for Meaning: An Introduction to Logotherapy* (New York, Washington Square Press, 1969).

Tool #8 – Retreat and Think Things Over

On "staying in the box," see Willliam E. Adams, Ph.D., *The Choices Program: How To Stop Hurting The People Who Love You* (Long Beach, California: William E. Adams, 2003).

On the Gottman research on flooding and DPA, see John M. Gottman, Ph.D., *Marital Therapy: A Research-Based Approach. Clinician's Manual.* (Seattle: The Gottman Institute, 2001.)

On the freeze-frame technique for self-soothing, see Doc Childre and Howard Martin, *The HeartMath Solution* (New York: Harper Collins, 1999).

About the Authors

Tony Fiore, Ph.D., is a California licensed psychologist, marriage therapist, and personal coach with clinical practices in Long Beach and Orange, California. He is a certified facilitator and trainer of both adult and adolescent anger management programs, a past Diplomat of the American Association of Anger Management Providers, and a Fellow in the American Institute of Stress.

Fiore often speaks to groups and organizations on stress and anger management. He is also a consultant to the workplace, conducting in-house stress management training to managers of small, medium, and family-owned businesses. He recently served as a script consultant to a popular TV show regarding anger management and publishes a popular monthly newsletter *Taming the Anger Bee*.

After graduating from Purdue University in 1972, he has been active in both community mental health, the private practice of psychology, and teaching, coaching, and writing for over 30 years. He has completed numerous certificate programs in the fields of psychology, coaching, and anger management. He has also received advanced training in marital therapy at the Gottman Institute in Seattle, Washington.

Ari Novick, Ph.D., is a certified facilitator and trainer in anger management and has a private practice in Laguna Beach, California. He is a diplomat of the American Association of Anger Management Providers and an associate member of the California Association of Marriage and Family Therapists. He is also a continuing education provider for the California Board of Behavioral Sciences and an approved anger management provider for the Orange County Department of Probation.

Novick has made numerous presentations on the subjects of anger management, stress management and empathy. He has been a consultant for both Discovery Channel and Fox Television. Novick is also a corporate consultant and conducts workshops and seminars for corporations in both the public and private sectors.

Novick received his bachelor's degree from the University of California at Santa Barbara and his master's degree from Pepperdine University. He recently completed his Ph.D. in Clinical Psychology at the California Graduate Institute.